On the Road in **Post-Revolutionary Mexico** with **Edward Weston** and **Tina Modotti**

Delancey Street Press
1133 Venice Blvd, Los Angeles, CA 90015
www.delanceystreetpress.com

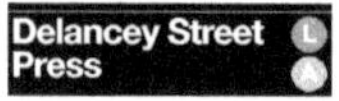

First edition
Library of Congress Cataloguing Publication Data Summary: A dual biography and critical assessment of Edward Weston and Tina Modotti

Includes footnotes
1. Biography 2. Photographic Criticism 3. Mexican History 4. European History
5. American History 6. Cultural History of the 20th Century

ISBN 979-8-234-01504-4
Printed in the United States of America

Book Design and Art Direction by Karen Davison

On the Road in **Post-Revolutionary Mexico** with **Edward Weston** and **Tina Modotti**

George Porcari

Contents

Introduction 9

Going to California 17

Leaving LA 33

A Revolution and a Renaissance 41

Aztec Land 49

Two Photographers Go to the Circus 65

A Marriage Portrait Without a Marriage 75

Mexico City Nights 87

Weston's Leaves of Grass 101

Weston Beach 109

In the Arsenal: Mella & Tinisíma 113

In Tehuantepec: A Greeting to Comrades 121

The Photography of Concern 127

The First Revolutionary Exhibition in Mexico! 133

Tina Modotti's War 141

Mexico City Undercover 159

Tina Visits an Old Friend and
Edward Remembers an Old Love 163

George Porcari 171

Endnotes 175

To Erika Espinoza

Patientia et Festivitas

Introduction

My first exposure to the work of Edward Weston was a retrospective exhibition in New York at MoMA in 1975. I was then living in Los Angeles but traveled to New York yearly hoping to move there at some point. I found that I strongly disliked Weston's work overall, as I was not then (or now) fond of formalism in photography, cinema or any other medium.

I did notice that his work from Mexico, especially the portraits and the portrait/nudes of Tina Modotti were superb – almost as if another person had done them. The pictures were daring and took unusual chances. They seemed to be knowledgeable about the more radical photographic work from Europe at the time but going their own independent way and having a great time doing it – they were playful, aggressive and complex. Ambiguity and contradiction were in the DNA of the work. I found this very odd as the latter work seemed polite, humorless, and one-note. I sought out explanations for how such great work produced in this short span of time in the 1920s could suddenly degenerate (from my perspective) into specious formalist clouds, plants and rocks. Even the later nudes were boring, which is saying something, as in 1975 I was 23 years old and rather liked nudes – then again, I was never interested in the "female form" but in women in a definite place, not a "space." In those early pictures from the 1920s Modotti is definitively in a place, the roof – the *azotea* – of a flat-roofed house in Mexico in the late afternoon. The official catalog for the show treated this early work as minor, a prelude of sorts to the main opera to come. Clearly, I had my work cut out for me.

My first exposure to Tina Modotti as someone other than Weston's model was the book by Mildred Constantine *Tina Modotti: A Fragile Life,* published in 1983, which I bought immediately. By then I was living in New York and working for the Strand bookstore and so had easy access to new books despite my meager pay. I was completely mesmerized by Modotti's work and her life story. Her work in its early phase resembled Weston's and I sought out Anita Brenner's book *Idols Behind Altars* that she and Weston had done together.

It was impossible to see any difference in their work, which opened up some questions that Constantine's book did not answer.

By coincidence another book, *Edward Weston in Mexico, 1923-1926,* by Amy Conger, was published the same year, 1983. While she mentions the similarities in their work she makes no attempt to explain it except to suggest that Modotti was an apprentice and so learning the ropes from the master she, of course, produced work similar to his. What this ignored is that Weston's work also changed in this period reflecting more of an avant-garde sensibility and Modotti eventually started to do more socially conscious documentary work completely outside of Weston's aesthetic worldview. Even more surprisingly there were a couple of pictures by Weston, of interior courtyard scenes that could easily have been done by Modotti in her more documentary style while her own still life photos were classic formalist studies that could have been done by Weston.

In 1984 I moved back to Los Angeles to get my MFA at the Art Center College in Pasadena, a suburb north of Los Angeles. By then Hayden Herrera's book on Frida Kahlo had made a celebrity of sorts of Frida. The book covers the Mexican Renaissance and the friendship between her and Modotti. The intersecting worlds that Kahlo, Modotti and the characters that made up the Mexican Renaissance created after the Revolution was a great read and furthered my understanding of Modotti and Weston's time in Mexico.

Later still, in 2010, when Anita Brenner's diaries and notebooks were published in a beautiful box edition with the wonderful title *Avant-Garde Art and Artists in Mexico: Anita Brenner's Journals of the Roaring Twenties,* I purchased them for the Art Center library – I had become the Acquisitions Librarian in the meantime and bought every biography of Modotti and Weston that came into print. That job not only saved my life but made it possible for me to check out books that I could not afford on my own, such as Brenner's journals.

In 2015 I published an essay in *CineAction* magazine titled *The Arc of a Dive: The Photography of Alexander Rodchenko and Leni Riefenstahl.* Although the two never met, by coincidence both had been photographing divers in pools 1934–1936 – all for the Olympic Games in Berlin. I realized that their pictures were at the opposite end of the spectrum photographically, politically and emotionally. This pairing of photographers seemed to hold a lot of promise in terms of writing about ideas and emotions as they present themselves photographically.

I had looked everywhere for answers but found none and realized I had to write this essay myself although I would have preferred if someone else had written it. Almost all of my work begins with that premise. The reason is that it only takes a few hours to read an essay but it can take a lifetime to write one. Finally, by 2023 I published my work on Tina Modotti and Edward Weston in a book of collected essays titled *One Second to Live: Photography, Film and the Corporeal in an Age of Extremes.* Unfortunately, I realized even before the book went to press that it had been a mistake to cut the essay down to fit the already sizable book. Rather it needed to be expanded into a book itself because the material was so rich and full of emotional twists, turns, dead ends and roundabouts – there was just so much rich photographic material to compare despite the relatively short six-year span of time they were together.

The essay started as strictly a study of their photography and I mentioned the lives of Weston and Modotti to fill in the time period, but slowly the lives started to become more important and take on more weight, as did the Mexican Revolution and the Mexican Renaissance that were so much a part of their lives. I liked to think that the book is evenly divided between critical assessment of photographs and biography with the scales just tipping toward photographic criticism, which is where I started – but as I saw when I counted it's the other way around. Nevertheless, the book at a certain point felt well balanced between biographical details, photographic criticism, and meaningful digressions and that is when I stopped – there were just the right number of notes.

I would like to acknowledge the books already mentioned as well as Margaret Hooks' enormously entertaining biography *Tina Modotti: Photographer and Revolutionary* as well as Patricia Albers' *Shadows, Fire, Snow: The Life of Tina Modotti.* The first does a superb job covering her undercover work in Europe and the latter her complicated friendships and love life in Los Angeles and Mexico. Sarah M. Lowe's *Tina Modotti & Edward Weston: The Mexico Years* is a wonderful large format photo book that has the best reproductions of their work and an excellent text that outlines their life and work together cogently and sympathetically. The best study of Weston's time in Los Angeles before he moved to Mexico is *Artful Lives: Edward Weston, Margrethe Mather, and the Bohemians of Los Angeles* by Beth Gates Warren. The book is large but Ms. Warren is a wonderful writer who writes history with a novelistic narrative flow making the reading a pleasure. Her book not only covers Weston's unusual relationship with Mather in detail but also does a great job with the avant-garde artists and bohemians of Los Angeles at the turn of the 20th century.

The best straight art history book about Weston or Modotti is by the brilliant art historian Mariana Figarella, *Edward Weston y Tina Modotti en Mexico: Su Inserción Dentro de las Estrategias Esteticas del Arte Postrevolucionario.* Unfortunately, the book is only available in a Spanish edition long out of print but worth the trouble to find. Ms. Figarella gets the work of both artists in lucid, jargon-free prose – there is brilliance in every page.

Elena Poniatowska's massive novel *Tinísima* is a vastly entertaining take not only on Tina but on many of the principal players in the Mexican Renaissance – in many cases these are people that Poniatowska knew or interviewed over the years. She brings a scathingly accurate, often comical, look at the world of Mexico City in the 1920s. The novel both looks back to the vast epic novels produced in the 19th century such as *Doña Perfecta* by Benito Pérez Galdós and looks forward to the more ironic comic/tragic works of Roberto Bolaño.

I would also like to thank Peter Wollen and Laura Mulvey, who made an extraordinary film, and accompanying catalog, titled *Frida Kahlo and Tina Modotti* that examined the work of both women from an invaluable feminist and poststructuralist critical perspective – while their film and subsequent catalog raised more questions than answers I consider that the greatest compliment I can pay them. In the 1970s Wollen introduced me to film theory with his wonderful book *Signs and Meaning in the Cinema* and he also wrote *The Passenger,* a film that I treasure and was fortunate enough to write about in my book on Michelangelo Antonioni, *The Antonioni Adventure*, published in 2019.

This book was not written with the help of any academic institution and I hope that this fact shows on every page, but I would like to thank the Art Center College Library, and their head librarian, for having hired me in 1989 and making my life so much easier and richer. Lastly, I would like to thank my family and friends who encouraged me through the long process, especially Veronica Gonzalez Peña, who was not only encouraging but was encouraged herself to begin to write her own novel about Tina Modotti – no doubt a subject that will live long after the labyrinthine and esoteric political struggles of the time are forgotten. As to the question that Weston asks in his *Daybooks* in 1942 when he hears of Modotti's death: "Will anyone remember Tina Modotti?" The answer is yes.

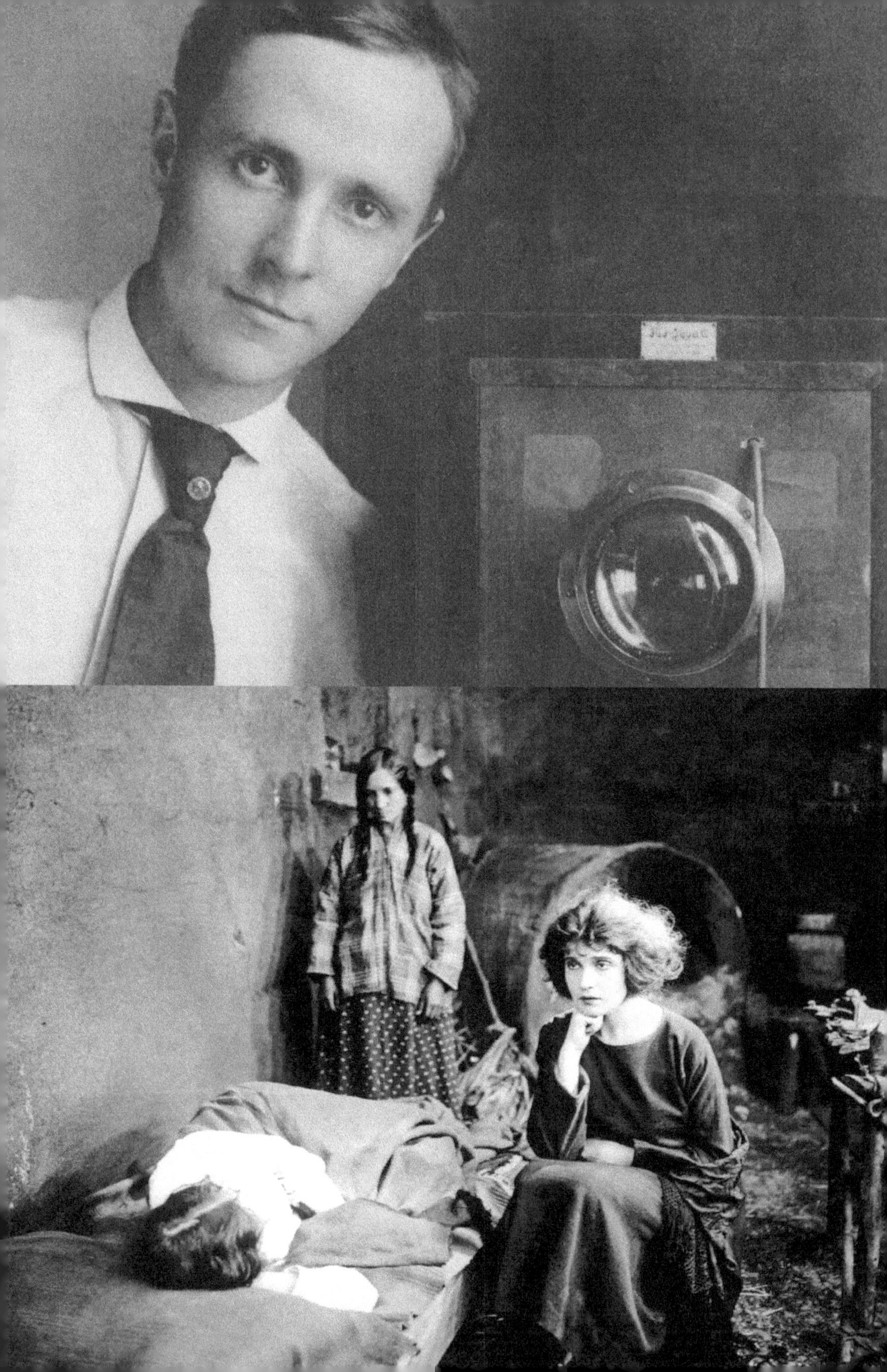

Something in the world forces us to think. This something is an object not of recognition but of a fundamental encounter. It may be grasped in a range of affective tones: wonder, love, hatred, suffering. In whichever tone, its primary characteristic is that it can only be sensed.

Gilles Deleuze, *Difference and Repetition*

The painter constructs, the photographer discloses.

Susan Sontag, *On Photography*

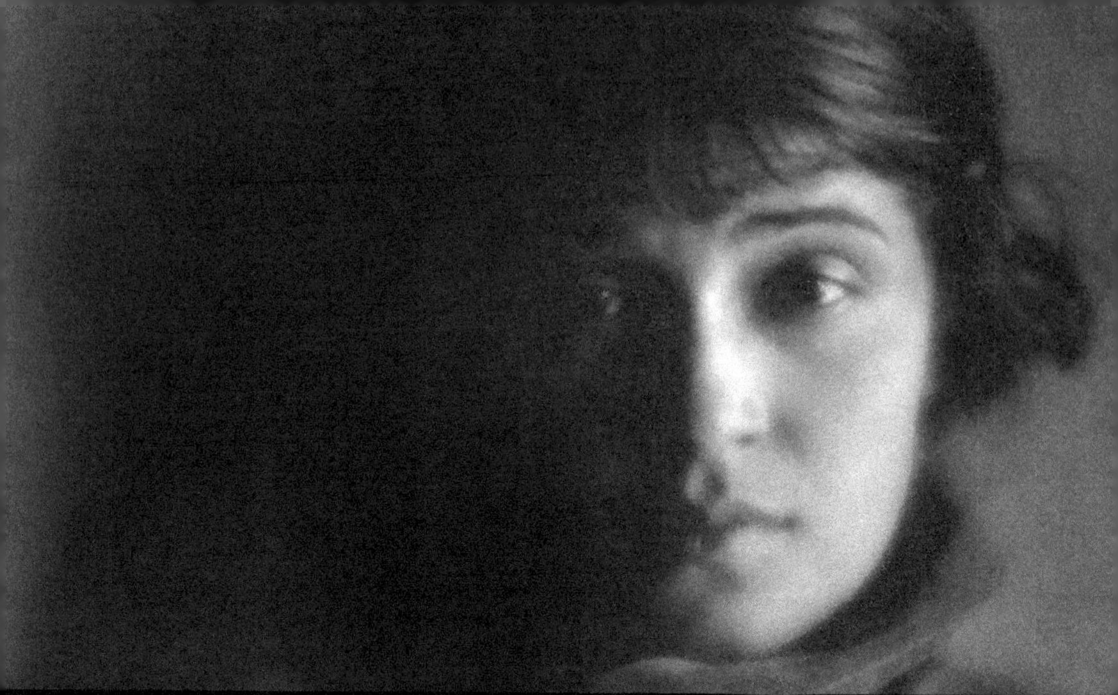

Made up my mind to make a new start…

Jimmy Page and Robert Plant, *Going to California*

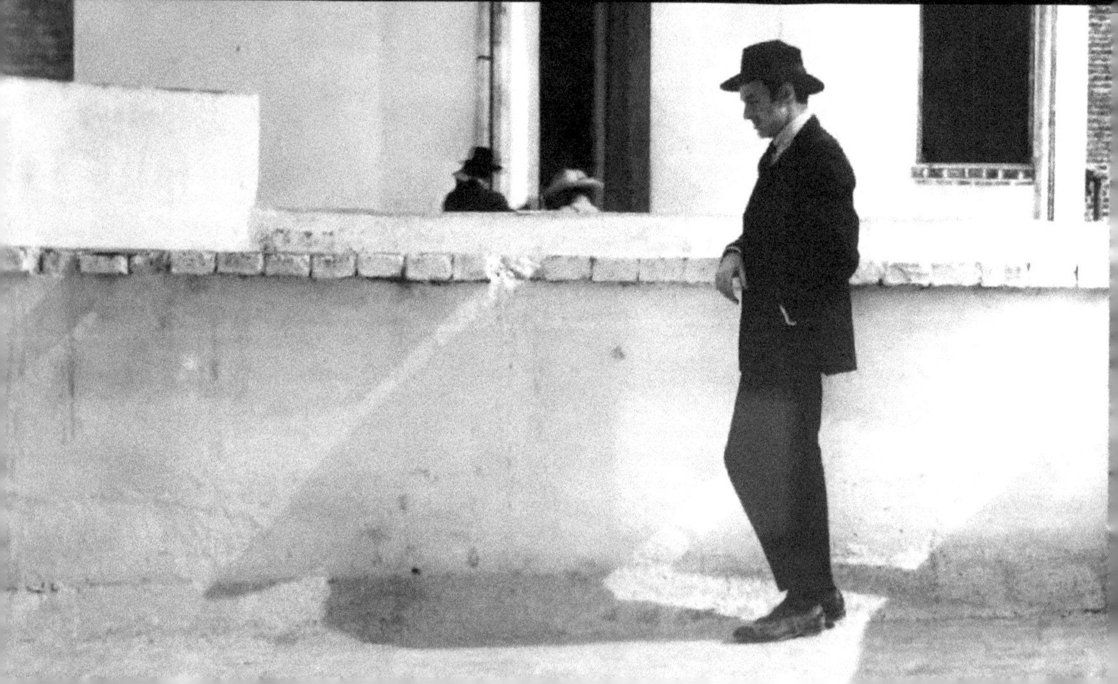

01

Going to California

Edward and Tina

By the time the 24-year-old actress/model Tina de Richey met the 34-year-old Edward Weston in Los Angeles in 1920 he was already a well-known photographer and highly regarded in his field. He was especially expert on technical matters with large-format cameras, lenses, and printing. Darkroom work then was a process akin to alchemical magic and he had his bag of tricks, and while some masters of the lab liked to keep their insider information a secret Weston was happy to share. He wrote regularly for photo journals, giving out practical hands-on advice but staying away from historical analysis and displaying indifference or hostility to theories. He was a pragmatist whose philosophical underpinnings were closer to the American writings of Ralph Waldo Emerson and William James than to any European schools, philosophically or photographically. In 1916 *Camera* magazine devoted a whole issue to his work. He also traveled regularly showing his work in galleries, and in 1917 he participated in a prestigious group exhibition in the London Salon of Photography.

By 1920–21 Tina de Richey, as Tina Modotti was called when Weston first knew her, was his lover, friend and photographic apprentice. As their relationship developed he taught her the historical foundations of the medium, from his perspective, providing her with the best available camera equipment at that moment, something she could not afford on her own. At the time Weston used a Graflex, a portable camera that produced a 3¼x4¼-inch negative and pinpoint focus, and an 11x14-inch view camera that needed a tripod, fitted with an 18-inch Wollensak Verito diffusing lens that allowed him to achieve soft-focus images with strong highlights, a style then in vogue for art photography.[1]

By the time they met this painterly photography, most often referred to as Pictorialism, was one that Weston was beginning to cautiously move away from, shifting toward a sharper focus, with an abstracted aesthetic that would at times come to be known as formalism or straight photography – movements that would develop a strong base in Europe and the US in the Twenties. Alfred

Stieglitz was the person who, with an open mind, debated the issue in his influential magazine *Camera Work* (1903–1917), and eventually shifted from Pictorialism to a formalist aesthetic under the effect of the work of Paul Strand and the ideas of Georgia O'Keeffe, two close friends.

It would be in Mexico under the influence of the muralists, principally Diego Rivera, that Weston would push the formalist style toward a small-scale monumentality – a contradiction in terms well suited to Weston's temperament – his first mature work. While formalism tended to abstract the photographic image into graphic points, lines and planes straight photography shied away from abstraction or painterly effects concentrating on the medium's ability to depict the present moment, stressing a direct confrontation with the thing itself. In straight photography there was presumably no staging, fakery or artsy effects of any kind, either in the camera or later in the darkroom. Nevertheless, in the real-world formalism and straight photography overlapped and Weston made work that shifted from one to the other, or contained elements of both, depending on the subject and even his mood. He was fundamentally an artist uninterested in ideologies or theories, considering them superfluous to the creation of his work. He believed that great art was made by "genius" existing outside the social norms or the pull of history, theories, or even technical skill, and while the latter might be essential it did not necessarily guarantee great work.

Weston credited Stieglitz for being at the forefront of photography taking full advantage of the medium's intrinsic qualities and leading the way in contemporary art photography. Stieglitz was acknowledged by many photographers and art historians as having taken the first modernist photograph, *The Steerage* (1907). The picture took advantage of an asymmetrical, open frame and a complex series of layers within the picture plane – with the primary subjects going in different directions at once rather than having a single static subject. An added appeal for Weston was that the picture reveled in its homegrown vitality and frenzy of activity, close in spirit to Walt Whitman's hymns to American Democratic vistas. *The Steerage* was clearly an American work of art. Weston was deeply inspired by the work as were many others. Stieglitz cast a large shadow over photography for decades and Weston's eventual meeting with him proved pivotal.

Weston slowly made that transition from Pictorialism to formalism, only a few steps behind Stieglitz, and he was Modotti's informal teacher. But as we will see the exchange of ideas between them eventually became a reciprocal one where each learned from the other in an intense and fruitful six-year partnership lasting from the end of 1920 to the end of 1926. The first three years of that association were spent in Los Angeles with the last three in Mexico City. They profoundly affected each other's work, pushing each other in ways that no one else could or would, and arguably each produced their best work during the three-year time frame that Weston referred to as his "Mexican period."

The reason for this has something to do with the two respective cities. In Los Angeles their accord was very much centered on the traditional artist/model relationship existing within a society of ambitious, anxious individualists jockeying for position in the marketplace and even in the hierarchy within the intersecting bohemian circles spread through the city. In Mexico they were a couple within a community of like-minded artists, writers, political activists and intellectuals that formed a creative collective. This society within a society in Mexico City – the avant-garde – was intent not merely to create beautiful work but to fundamentally change society for the better by creating a more egalitarian, humanistic world order without national or economic boundaries.

In that sense much of the writing and the artwork from this period was a means to utopia or some Edenic end to history. The work has much in common with religious art where beauty, as such, was merely a byproduct. The end was religious instruction or indoctrination that engendered feelings of metaphysical illumination – vague feelings that would find voice and direction in religious orthodoxy. For many artists and writers within the avant-garde circles of this period one substitutes Marxism for Christianity – in both cases there was a master plan. Later, after the fall of the Soviet Union, capitalism would take up this crusade to find Eden – most famously with Francis Fukuyama's The End of History and the Last Man (1992) arguing that capitalism/democracy had now created conditions worldwide signaling the endpoint of humanity's social and political evolution. In the thirties Communism promised this evolution and seemed to have victory, as the writer Mario Vargas Llosa put it, "just around the corner."

They were called "Edward and Tina" by their Mexico City friends, who took for granted that they were a working team of professionals as well as a couple – in a sense they became a foreign version of "Diego and Frida." It is not surprising that the four became good friends despite the fact that Weston never managed to learn Spanish and Diego Rivera never learned English despite his long periodic stays in New York. The two couples also lived close by in Mexico City. Modotti spoke Spanish fluently, but with an American accent and an Italian lilt in certain words that were similar to Italian – people found it difficult to place her. Tina was more social, more used to a Latin sensibility from her childhood in Italy, and Weston came to depend on her not only as a translator but emotionally – anywhere they had to go that involved groups of people he wanted her close by. Mexico equalized them in a sense – it was no longer a master/apprentice relationship and Modotti took full advantage as her work, not surprisingly, blossomed in the new setting.

Idols Behind Altars

There was a reciprocal exchange of ideas in their work, which reached a point where their pictures became so similar it was difficult for people at the time to tell them apart. This fusion reached its apex in 1926 when Anita Brenner commissioned Weston and Modotti, who by then was his official assistant, to take photographs for her groundbreaking book *Idols Behind Altars: Modern Mexican Art and Its Cultural Roots*.

The basic thesis of the book was, first, that in Mexico behind the iconic Spanish Colonial Catholic paintings and altars lay the pagan idols of Aztec and Mayan cultures – a feature referred to as syncretism. In that sense these religious icons and paintings contained pagan iconography and one could read these works as a palimpsest with various meanings overlaid. For example, in Christian iconography a snake is a symbol of evil, knowledge and temptation but in Aztec mythology a snake is a symbol of rebirth and fertility – Mexican artists managed to combine both symbols simultaneously so the painting could be read either way. This same syncretism was seen in South America, particularly in Peru and the Cuzco school of artists who became masters of syncretism – a secret coded language of pictorial art.

The second theme of Brenner's book was that she made the connection (then new) that contemporary Mexican artists and muralists had taken this syncretism further, fusing the complex iconography of precolonial and colonial art into grand symphonic narratives that brought the work into contemporary times, with figures working in factories, cities, etc. Of course, in this new layering of meanings the muralists were not using a secretive code as the connections they made between Aztecs, Christian martyrs, and exploited industrial workers was blatantly clear. Brenner's arguments for a syncretism within Catholic iconography and contemporary art was then relatively new but has since become an influential theme within academic art history, with links to identity politics and cultural studies.

The book also followed the lead of the *indigenismo* movement in Mexico. This controversial ideology expressed the idea that indigenous people were the "quintessential Mexicans" as they had, despite enormous social pressure and violence, resisted European culture, maintaining ties to folk traditions secretly or through some form of syncretism. There was a heroic aspect to *indigenismo* – a cultural movement that the muralists, as well as many intellectuals, writers and poets, gravitated to primarily by focusing on the nobility, resistance and strength of the working class. One problem that arose was that many well-educated artists, writers, etc., did not belong to the working class but looked up to its members as "symbols" of resistance and solidarity – this created a gap between them that never came together, finally turning into an unbridgeable abyss by 1968. While Modotti responded positively to *indigenismo* Weston found that much of the work of the avant-garde, particularly Dada-inspired manifestos and the more conceptual work, was nonsense – a "glass-bead game" for intellectuals. This was the attitude of a great many people outside of the artistic circles and the intellectual class that made up the Mexican Renaissance.

While Weston chose to ignore *indigenismo* because of his mistrust of any ideology or theory, Modotti joined in and after 1926–27 focused her public photographic work almost exclusively on workers, accentuating the noble or heroic aspect of their condition or their poverty in the face of enormous wealth disparity. In this respect her work anticipates the photography of the *WPA* in the US and the photojournalism in Europe during the 1930s that found cogent subject matter in the struggle of the working classes and the fight against oligarchs and fascism that we can see in the work of Ramón Masats, Gerda Taro, and Robert Capa among others.

Incredibly Brenner herself was only 21 when in 1926 she paid $1,000 to Weston to travel through Mexico and take pictures of certain art objects, archeological sites and contemporary murals that she had drawn up in a long list. The commission would mean two months of constant travel, in many cases to places only reachable at that time with horses and pack mules.[2] Brenner's list was not a simple shopping list of items but an eight-page, single spaced catalog of items such as "Mexican Decorative Arts" that was then subdivided into Sarapes, Rebozos, Fajas, Bolsas, Embroidery, etc. These in turn were further subdivided into places such as Michoacan, Tehuantepec, Jalisco, etc.[3] The negatives had to be carefully labeled so when they were eventually printed the information could be written on the back of each picture. Weston/Modotti were up to the heavy detail work and Brenner was thrilled with the result.

Anita Brenner was a Jewish scholar and intellectual who would help not only Weston and Modotti but a host of others during this period. Born in Aguascalientes, Mexico, and raised in Texas, she left the US when she turned 18, due in part to the anti-Semitism she experienced in her university years in Texas. She returned to Mexico City and its strong Jewish diaspora community where she finally felt accepted and began to explore not only her own Jewish roots but also those of the Mexican community around her.[4] She published the first book on the Mexican Revolution, still in print, and she coined the term "Mexican Renaissance" to describe the cultural florescence that emerged after the Revolution. This was a group that she helped to foster, to promote and to historicize.

Brenner's commission was also a great opportunity for Weston and Modotti to explore Mexico in depth, take their own pictures and get paid for it. Upon receiving the approximately 200 prints Brenner was unable to tell the difference between their respective pictures as the images were unsigned – only the description and place names were listed. This confusion as to authorship did not bother Brenner in the least as she considered the photographs merely illustrations to her text. She ended up using 70 of the photographs in her seminal book, finally published in 1929, but by then Weston was already back in California and Modotti was in the final months of her stay before moving to Europe. Some radical coalescence of the Weston/Modotti aesthetic trajectory had taken place between 1920 and 1926 to the extent that a young but knowledgeable art historian could not tell the difference between their work. What happened?

Their friends noticed this confluence in their pictures, this inability to see where one body of work began and the other ended, and teased them about it but did not pursue it further. In 1983 when Amy Conger published a catalog for a show at the San Francisco Museum of Modern Art titled *Edward Weston in Mexico: 1923–1926* she took notice. While Conger mentions *Idols Behind Altars* and the inability of Brenner to tell the difference (or care) she does not pursue it further either.[5] Helpfully she does quote Brenner in one of her letters long after the fact, from 1965: "Tina did a good deal of the work interchangeably with Edward so that it would be impossible really to say whose pictures are which."[6] Most writers, including Conger, describe Modotti as merely Weston's assistant, which suggests someone who carries camera equipment, loads film and perhaps occasionally cooks dinner.

Brenner would also use some of the photographs by Weston/Modotti in the magazine *Mexico This Month* that was edited by Brenner and while she captioned the photographs with the correct location and subject matter – provided by Weston/Modotti – she credited both photographers for all of the pictures in the acknowledgments, thereby solving the problem by avoiding it altogether. This seems to have been the way most people handled the question.[7] Brenner justified this decision by pointing out that she had paid for the work and so the pictures belonged to her. Later, when Modotti subsequently tried to sell some of her pictures in Europe when she was strapped for cash, it caused a temporary rift between them, but they remained friends.

This book will devote itself to some basic questions that arise from the discussion thus far: What happened to the work of Edward Weston and Tina Modotti between 1920 and 1926 that there was such a pronounced merging of their pictorial sensibility and aesthetic? Why did this confluence in their photography shift both of their work toward the avant-garde? Why did they decide to move to Mexico City if neither of them had ever been there before? Why did the collaboration abruptly end? Lastly, what happened to them and to their photography after their time together?

Edward Weston Gets a Job

Weston was born in the small town of Highland Park, Illinois, which is both very close and very far from Chicago. His mother was an actress who died when he was five, probably causing a lasting trauma in the family as he retained a vivid memory of her on her deathbed. Weston was fostered in this Christian middle-class neighborhood by his older sister and this relationship proved to be his strongest and most long-lasting family connection.

In the summer of 1902 Weston's father sent 16-year-old Edward a gift of a Kodak Bulls Eye #2 camera that produced 3½-inch negatives. His first photograph was of chickens, taken on his aunt's farm.[8] Weston was fortunate in that he found his passion early and pursued it, almost religiously, for the remainder of his life. Other interests left him indifferent in comparison. His only training was a short stint at the Illinois School of Photography but Weston was not cut out for academic discipline or formal studies. His first job was at the Chicago department store Marshall Fields, where he realized that he needed to leave Chicago and start a new life elsewhere. His like-minded sister had recently moved to Los Angeles and that seemed promising, as the city traditionally offered a fresh start.

Mr. Modotti Moves to San Francisco

The Modottis came from Udine, Italy. Modotti's father, Giuseppe, was a mason and a mechanic and her mother, Assunta, a seamstress. The working-class family had traveled to Austria for a few years doing migrant work and Tina had learned to speak German fluently. The family eventually returned to Udine where Modotti got a job in a textile factory, often going hungry as there was not enough money for regular meals. Tina also caught typhoid fever that left her fragile – she never forgot the poverty of those early years. Giuseppe was also a radical, firebrand union organizer who finally emigrated to California in 1906 bringing the family over one at a time over a span of years – a normal custom at the time for immigrant laborers. Giuseppe's brother Pietro had a successful photography studio in Italy and this is where Tina would have been introduced to the photographic process and to the idea that one could make a living from photography.

Modotti boarded a ship from Genoa to New York at the age of 16 on July 8, 1913. Tina – the nickname of Assunta Adelaide Luigia Modotti Mondini – measuring just over five feet, was officially documented as a "student" by the immigration officials at Ellis Island and allowed into New York. Her mother's name was also Assunta so she was called Assuntina (little Assunta) but at a certain point Assuntina became just Tina. Her final destination was Taylor Street in the Russian Hill area of San Francisco. This move was emblematic of her peripatetic life to come. Modotti would eventually live in eight countries in her 45 years, and come to speak four languages, all of them with a slight accent, as if she was never at home. She lived, as Latin Americans say, with her bags always ready.

Modotti immediately took well to the Bay Area's vital immigrant cosmopolitan culture with an array of languages, visual styles and open markets, similar to Italy. While poverty was prevalent it existed alongside a strong middle class and pockets of wealth in adjacent Nob Hill. Bohemia and the city also had a long history that she would join as she grew older. It was the perfect place for Modotti to transform from an immigrant seamstress who occasionally modeled for department stores – then an accepted norm in upscale shops – to a theater actress. She was theatrical by nature and took well to being onstage, using the highly expressive and accentuated style of acting then in fashion. Within a short time she had a career as an actress and received some good reviews for her work in the local paper, even developing a following. Acting seemed to be a promising profession, with all of the new theaters in San Francisco opening up after the earthquake in 1906 and the burgeoning film industry in Los Angeles, a city that was only a few hours away by train on the coast.

Modotti's plunge into theater was not a hobby or a pastime but a heartfelt deep dive into regional theater as a first step to a career in acting. Regional theater is long gone and hard to grasp now but productions were in the original language of the region, in Modotti's case the plays were in Italian; the writing, directing and acting were done by local people who were often pulled off the street for tryouts. Works were melodramatic, tending to be operatic, sentimental and in tune with current events. Larger, more prestigious "legitimate theater" companies looked to regional theater for young talent, as did the film industry in Hollywood. Frank Puglia, a fellow actor in Modotti's company, moved to Hollywood and became a well-known successful character actor – he was an inspiration to many others.[9] Producers and directors in Los Angeles made the trip to San Francisco to spot talent or a fresh face, most famously D.W. Griffith, who came in 1918. Unfortunately, Griffith and Modotti never met, as it would have been interesting to know what Tina thought of the puritanical Kentuckian who discovered Lilian Gish. Hollywood people were looking not only for actors but for material to transpose to film as the need for new stories was constant and competitive – the entertainment business in Hollywood was becoming a major industry. Modotti had good reasons for being confident.

Tropico/Los Angeles

By the turn of the century Weston's older sister had already settled in Los Angeles and found a job. He arrived there in 1906 at the age of 20, moving to Tropico (now Glendale). Shortly thereafter he married one of his sister's friends, Flora May Chandler, who belonged to one of the wealthiest families in the city that controlled substantial real estate interests and the city's major newspaper, *The Los Angeles Times*. Ms. Chandler was bourgeois, strict, stern and conventional, all of the things that Weston had sought to escape from when he left Chicago. He very clearly also seemed to have had a psychological need for it, as this propriety was an umbilical cord that he would never escape.

As the biographer Patricia Albers more bluntly put it: "She [Flora Chandler] loved him deeply and he found her both infuriating and indispensably generous with money."[10]

In 1910 Weston opened his own photographic studio in Glendale specializing in soft-focus Pictorialist works with the romantic themes and symbols that constituted his personal work of the time. For money he also photographed traditional family sittings and portraits. He was relatively successful at it on all accounts though he had profound misgivings about his commercial work and its relation to art photography – he carefully set about destroying most of this work after the fact. Like many young artists he was searching for his own voice, and to make room for his work in the history of the medium. Weston was not helped by the fact that he generally felt out of place in avant-garde circles finding the political rhetoric and discussions of art theory pointless.

Bohemian enclaves with hopeful avant-garde artists were plentiful in Los Angeles at the turn of the century but scattered and disconnected. An artist from Silver Lake might live in the city for years and never meet another artist from Chavez Ravine, only a few miles away – artists and writers were not able to build a cohesive community over time as they did in New York or Paris. Nevertheless, Los Angeles was a mecca for people searching for a more off-the-grid relaxed lifestyle without the Puritan emphasis on work, religion and family. It was a magnet for artists, misfits and slackers – the term used then for men avoiding the army – all looking for some shelter from the storms of the marketplace and the dominant culture. The Los Angeles of that time was a place where one could drown out the noise and find oneself. The city is ecologically a desert so had warm breezes during the day and cool nights. It was the beginning of L.A.'s love affair with the automobile, and hot jazz on Central Avenue centered around the Dunbar Hotel where mixed races mixed freely. There were oil derricks everywhere including the beautiful beaches and they were loud, smelly and filthy. There were marathon dance contests and it was the beginning of the flapper, the first liberated woman who proclaimed it openly and unashamedly. The Twenties were when the main personality points of the "lost generation," that is, solid ethics, an ability to see through hype and bullshit and contempt for mainstream mores and culture, were trickling down to young middle-class men and women as a kind of soft cynicism. It was a moment when many in the Hollywood community, including the writers recently arrived from New York, mixed freely with the bohemians and artists living in the dilapidated Victorian houses in the hills of downtown, with a heavy emphasis on dancing, alcohol, and long talks into the night.

Pictorialism and Alfred Stieglitz

When pictures of everyday life first appeared in the late 19th and early 20th century, by photographers such as August Zille, Eugene Atget and Erich Salomon, they were in the minority and attracted little attention. Most photographers who considered themselves serious or professional were using the medium as a means to an end. They saw photography as a helpful tool in the sciences or as a means to produce high art, be it classically staged tableaux or Impressionist landscapes, the two dominant fine-art styles of the late 19th century – this was a format known as Pictorialism.

Pictorialists, such as Alfred Steiglitz, Gertrude Käsebier, Alvin Langdon Coburn, as well as the young Weston, carefully followed the rigid program of composition and effects laid out by painting in order that their photographs might be considered fine art. Pictorialism was a photographic movement that was heavily promoted by Alfred Stieglitz's magazine *Camera Work* in its early years during the Belle Epoque. This group often used special lenses and gels, along with atmospheric effects, and manipulated prints with soft focus to simulate painting, as the photographic print was by then very sharp, with a lot of detail – the contingent world of real life – usually not found in paintings. For Pictorialists the point was not details or clarity in the print, or even the reproduction of reality, but to create a work of art. The often-repeated motto of photographers that practiced some form of Pictorialism was: "The business of a work of art is to make an effect, not to report a fact. Otherwise...the camera has no more artistic potentiality than a gas meter."[11]

Despite Weston's allegiance to Pictorialism he never had a "school" that he belonged to per se or a theory that he subscribed to and sought to illustrate. Rather his work from its earliest stages when he was a teenager onward was intuitive and always gravitated towards finding patterns in nature. Weston loved correspondences and biomorphic, mutable forms seen from the right angle, the right lighting. In a sense his pictures were created twice, once in the world at large when they were found and again later in the darkroom when they were re-created in black and white. His work was consistent throughout his life and one can find correspondences. For example, Graham Howe and R.D. Beth Warren, in their fine book *Edward Weston: Portrait of the Artist as a Young Man*, pair off a shot of Santa Monica Bay from 1910 with an eerily "oceanic" but actually desert view from Death Valley in 1937. Despite the 27 year span here is a similar concern with natural forms in constant flux – Weston had an archeological sense of time where everything was intriguingly mutable and fluid – a metamorphosis of ever-changing forms captured/created by the artist with a camera.

By the time Weston took up photography as a profession Pictorialism seemed, even to Stieglitz who was one of the founders of the movement, out of touch. Something new was called for – why? The Parisian art dealer who helped put Cubism (1907 to the early 1920s) on the map, D.H. Kahnweiler offers some answers:

> I lived those seven crucial years from 1907 to 1914 with my painter friends... what occurred at that time in the plastic arts will be understood only if one bears in mind that a new epoch was being born, in which man (all mankind in fact) was undergoing a transformation more radical than any other known within historical times.[12]

When Virginia Woolf was looking back on the transition in society from her youth in the 1890s to the 1930s, she said something very similar, that is, that civilization and "the human character as a whole had changed decisively sometime in December of 1910."[13] Being a true modernist Woolf was being serious and ironic at the same time. It seemed like the older forms in the plastic arts, music, poetry, etc., regardless of how good they were, could not describe this new period. One needed Cubism, Dada, Futurism, Constructivism – the harsh displacements within the tonal scale of Stravinsky, Shostakovich and Schoenberg – the radical disjunctions and parodies of James Joyce, Apollinaire and Eliot – in short one needed a form that could keep up. Everyone arrived at this exhortation from Ezra Pound to "make it new" in a different way. Some arrived through painstaking study, some through instinctive perception, some through pure will and hard work, and some through sheer disgust – but they got there.

How did photography respond to this revolution? It didn't. For the most part it ignored it, for the basic reason that it didn't have to pay attention. For most people the primary function of photography was seen as utilitarian – making resemblances – or making photographs that resembled the art of the past. But there were people scattered across Europe and Russia who were pushing photography to deal with this new world described by Woolf and Kahnweiler such as Alexander Rodchenko and Max Alpert in Moscow, Germaine Krull and Umbo in Berlin, and Man Ray and Brassai in Paris among others. These were artists who were shifting the ground under photographic history but they were in Europe and Russia, far from Weston's studio in Glendale.

By the teens Weston was producing romantic, soft-focus photographs but he suspected that he had reached an aesthetic cul-de-sac as the form was clearly not up to dealing with the contemporary urban realities of Los Angeles at the turn of the century. Like many artists he grew frustrated – certainly the plastic work of the Cubists and Futurists that he was familiar with from reproductions were all "new" but how to apply those lessons to photography? For example, the work by the Italian Futurists that Weston saw in San Francisco in 1915 was clearly traditional and modern at the same time, that is, all of art history seemed to be in those paintings but they were also completely of the moment, urban, radical – but was it even possible to do that with a photograph? Weston reasoned that there must be a way.

A new direction was provided in part by the 291 Gallery in New York that had been opened by Stieglitz in 1905. There he showed a wide variety of artists from all ages, locations and genres, often at the same time, in extensive and well-attended group shows. Stieglitz exhibited old masters alongside younger painters, sculptors, avant-garde artists and traditionalists, as well as work by photographers from all over the United States – he shied away from the radical work being done in Europe and Russia, showing and promoting homegrown talent. His idea was that if you showed a wide range of work people could develop their own ideas. From the time it opened on Fifth Avenue in Manhattan a trip to the 291 Gallery for a photographer was tantamount to visiting a holy shrine and Stieglitz was its high priest who might bless a young acolyte by introducing him or her to the right crowd or through participation in a group show. In 1922 Weston traveled to New York City to meet the master photographer from Hoboken, New Jersey – he was not disappointed.

Weston showed his portfolio concentrating on his portraits along with his first sharp-focus works of steel factories in Ohio. The two men poured over the photographs and spent several hours in conversation. Stieglitz was impressed by Weston's passion and by his work, exclaiming in a letter: "Your work and attitude reassures me. You have shown me at least several prints which have given me a great deal of joy. And I can seldom say that of photographs."[14] While in Manhattan Weston also met Charles Sheeler and saw his early sharp focus formalist work of grain silos and factories. Along with Stieglitz they talked over the new photos and their differentiation from strict (non-art) documentation. Weston returned from New York to Los Angeles with a fresh fervor for the medium and he set down to work.

Robo

Both Weston and Modotti found mates early in their lives but they decided on very different people. Modotti chose a man named Roby Richey, originally a farm boy from Oregon, who had come to San Francisco to reinvent himself as an exotic artist named Robo de l'Abrie Richey. Robo was something of a manqué bohemian, dressed in the style of a romantic European artist from an earlier period in Prince Albert jackets and velvet smocks. His attention span seems to have never settled between designing batiks, painting, writing poetry or illustration. Robo immersed himself in the artistic and belletristic literary life of San Francisco hoping to make a name for himself – he was simultaneously naïve and sophisticated, narcissistic and full of self-doubt, an aesthete who never finished anything but always dreamed big. Modotti seems to have been irresistibly drawn to Robo's passion for art and his contempt for moneymaking, the "herd mentality," traditional status symbols, and bourgeois respectability.

They met at the Panama-Pacific International Exposition in 1915, the San Francisco World's Fair that celebrated the opening of the Panama Canal and the city's reconstruction following the 1906 earthquake. The Fair was a chance for San Franciscans to see the new art from other American cities, principally New York, and the new Post-Impressionist and Expressionist art from Europe. Weston had his photographic work in the massive show where he was in the American photography wing of the exhibit that Modotti must surely have seen. He had traveled by train to San Francisco to see the fair but he and Modotti never met as they attended on different days but both were impressed by the new paintings of Edvard Munch and the Italian Futurists who were seen in the US for the first time.[15] Modotti did meet Robo at the fair and they quickly became an inseparable couple – they married and moved together to Los Angeles in 1918 so Modotti could pursue her career as an actress in Hollywood – a logical step up from the small theaters in San Francisco. This is Patricia Albers describing Modotti in this period:

> Whether it was painting, poetry or American cooking, whatever the young Tina deemed worthy of attention, she absorbed with a single-minded focus. The pair [Robo and Tina] went on to explore an undigested mix of contemporary thinkers, skimming Freud, Oscar Wilde...Nietzsche was fashionable in the 1920's bohemia but Tina was more profoundly marked than most by her reading of him. She accepted his ideas about the vital importance of making art. She also retained the notions that one must, at all costs, avoid a herd mentality, live on one's own terms and decide for oneself what constitutes happiness.[16]

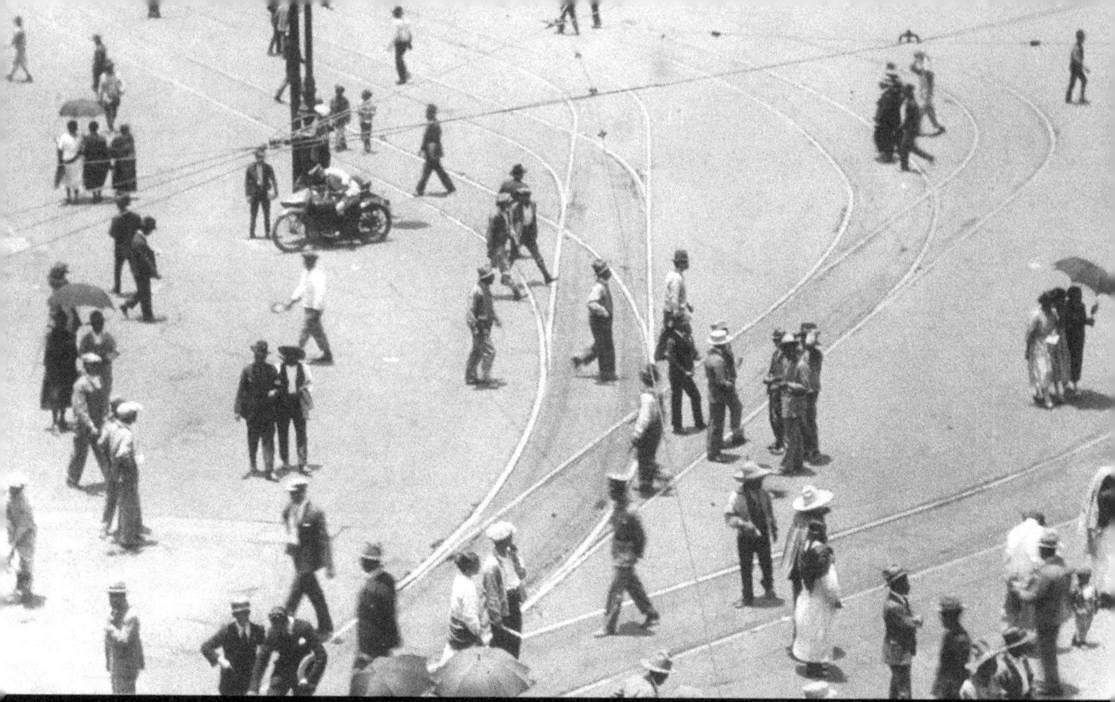

The sun is a joke.

Nathaniel West, *The Day of the Locust*

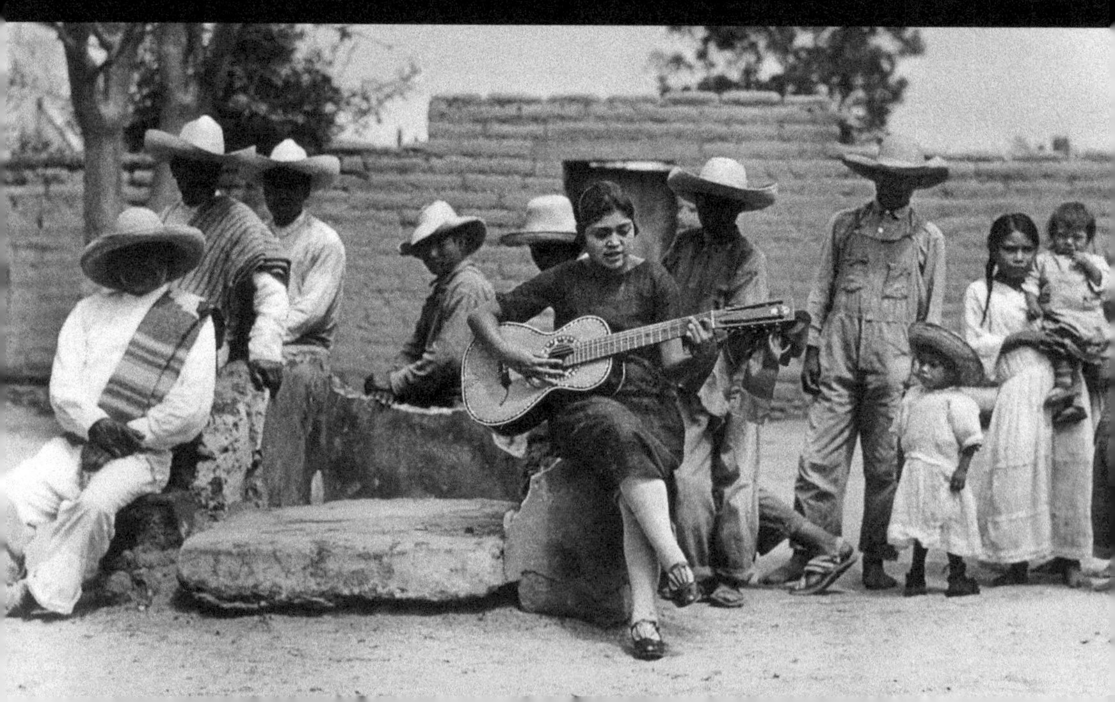

02

Leaving LA

Margrethe Mather

How had Weston, who in 1912 was photographing traditional family portraits and soft-focus landscapes, manage to transform himself within 10 years so that when he visited New York in 1922 his work was favorably looked upon by Alfred Stieglitz? The short answer to that question is Margrethe Mather. Sometime in 1913 the 27- year-old Mather – a self-taught photographer – visited Weston's Los Angeles studio to examine his work and see what the fuss was all about. It was to be a life-altering visit for both of them.

Mather was a bohemian in the strict sense of the term, that is, she lived free of contemporary mores and conventions for the sake of art, beauty and the pursuit of pleasure without giving much thought to the practical necessities of day-to-day living. Mather was the real thing – she didn't pursue any of the affectations of bohemian high culture for their own sake – she simply followed her own instincts for better and for worse. Not only was she flamboyant and bisexual, but her permissive sexuality and openness to experimentation in photography and avant-garde art collided with Weston's more conventional, cautious lifestyle and photography. Mather in a sense opened the door to avant-garde practice for Weston as he felt comfortable talking with her. The reasons were clear since she had no overall plan, theory or manifesto. As in her life so with her photography, she simply flew by the seat of her pants, and Weston responded to that instinctual directive.

This is Beth Gates Warren, writing about the bohemian enclave of Los Angeles in the period that Weston and Mather would have known:

> Many gravitated to accommodations in dilapidated Victorian-era boarding houses that populated the heights of downtown's Bunker Hill; others to rustic bungalows strewn across the hillsides of nearby Echo Park and Silver Lake. Although these individuals lived hand-to-mouth and moment-to-moment, they pursued their dreams and enjoyed their lives. They became the bohemians

> of Los Angeles, living unusual and often artistic lives. They were people like bookseller Jake Zeitlin, artist Paul Landacre, architect Rudolf Schindler, author Raymond Chandler, photographers Edward Weston and Margrethe Mather, and actors Charlie Chaplin, Rudolph Valentino, and Boris Karloff. All resided within the city's bohemian neighborhoods and often found themselves going down parallel (and occasionally intersecting) paths.[17]

Weston was dumbstruck and infatuated by Mather's work and by her – he had never seen or met anyone like her. In effect she became Weston's photographic mentor, but they did not have a sexual relationship as Mather was primarily a lesbian. True to style Weston never tired of trying to persuade her to give heterosexuality (and him) a chance. Nevertheless, they grew emotionally close and dependent on each other. When Weston finally decided to leave the country and relocate to Mexico a few years later she begged him to stay.

Mather's work was starkly modernist, severe and angular. Her major stylistic trademark was that she left large sections of the frame empty with a radical use of negative space that dominated her obsessive framing. It was as if she was pushing photography toward a minimalist aesthetic that did not yet exist. Her sense of play reduced three-dimensional space into abstract patterns that often had an Art Deco flavor, then in style. This radical use of space was something that would be done by avant-garde European photographers only years later in the 1920s. While many who saw Mather's pictures were simply puzzled Weston immediately saw their power and modernity.

It was clear that Mather was ahead of the game with her more radical minimalist work – with her Weston seemed to finally find his own way, coming to use hard diagonals in a more aggressive way with strong negative spaces that sometimes came forward as positive spaces receded. He found he had a gift for pictorial ambiguity and play. Very soon he had caught up with Mather and they were producing strong modernist works. Weston's portraits in particular became engaged in this formalist play in a very pronounced way under Mather's influence.

Weston copied not only Mather's style but also her subject matter switching from romantic landscapes and moody portraits to Mather's primary subjects (by her own admission): "hands, eggs, melons, waves, bathroom fixtures, seashells and bird wings."[18] These are all subjects that he would adopt and make his own through constant application for the remainder of his life.[19]

Mather also had a penchant for falling in love with a particular style, pursuing it, and when it was over and done with she would move on. For example, when the pedantic but influential art critic Antony Anderson started to cultivate a relationship with Weston – tolerating Mather as a female hanger-on – he impressed upon the young photographer the importance of James McNeill Whistler as an artist. Whistler's work was seen by many critics of the period as a more sophisticated, droll and urbane version of the French Post-Impressionists who were deemed too vulgar and crude; soon Weston and Mather were both making work inspired by the American painter – perhaps to court Anderson or maybe they did fall under Whistler's spell. Weston even did a photograph of his elderly father in 1917 that resembled Whistler's iconic painting of his mother, while Mather around the same time made *Pierrot*, a Whistler-like photo that contrasts an actor wearing a Pierrot outfit at the bottom right of the frame with a large theatrical tassel at the top left while the center of the image is a blank wall that seems to become an empty space – by then this disturbing emptiness was a Mather trademark. Their Whistler-inspired work looked very similar and they were clearly thinking as a unit; they also used each other as models dressing up in costumes with suggestive artistic or cinematic poses.

Whistler was an advocate of an art-for-arts-sake, apolitical ideology that would have been amenable to both Weston and Mather, but their Whistler detour was preempted by photography's turn to a sharp-focused aesthetic announced by Charles Sheeler, Paul Strand and other modern masters – even the pragmatic Stieglitz eventually came around. It was not simply a matter of sharp details but of philosophic outlook. Strand reasoned that photography was an art form that need not look toward any other art – the photographic negative was sharp and highly detailed and then so be it. Mather's and Weston's forays into Whistler's Aesthetic Movement was the last gasp of photographic Pictorialism before the acceptance of a more radical, modernist, graphic style that they would shortly adopt, again as a unit.

When Weston photographed *Ruth Shaw* (1922) it was clear he had not only absorbed Mather's techniques but was playing with oblique framing and abstract shapes, using them as a counterpoint to the human face and body that in Ruth Shaw's case is barely visible as only a small part of her head peeks out from the bottom of the picture assuming Mather's use of the same formal technique. *Ruth Shaw* also succeeds in doing something generally absent from Mather's work – it adds a sense of humor. Mather was an austere Calvinist in her work (if not her life) – almost as if she were articulating an Amish style of photography. In Weston's picture Shaw, at the very bottom of his frame, appears to be just exiting the picture altogether leaving only graphic shapes. The picture is playful, dynamic, aggressive and self-assured. Weston had found his voice and, almost as importantly, he knew it.

At the peak of their relationship in 1921 Weston and Mather entered into a semiformal partnership, showing their work together with both of them signing all of the prints their studios produced regardless of who had made the work. This is the only time in Weston's long career that he shared credit with another photographer by cosigning prints. As with the Weston/Modotti collaboration for Brenner's book – where the prints were unsigned – many admirers found it impossible to tell whose work was Weston's and whose pictures were Mather's. Both photographers seem to have been amused by the situation and they never told.

Unfortunately for Mather her style was dictated by intuitive reasoning and she never seems to have found a way to explore those empty spaces further and push her work to see where it might lead. Predictably as Mather grew older her work did not grow, her bohemian coterie became smaller, and her finances, her health and her photographic interests declined. After Weston's later success in middle age Mather took a more jaundiced view of her own work and Weston's fame. Aside from having given up photography, in her infrequent letters in later years she claimed to no longer want her older work exhibited and preferred to be forgotten. Mather's wish was not granted as in 2001 the Santa Barbara Museum of Art mounted an exhibition, with an accompanying catalog written by Beth Gates Warren titled *Margrethe Mather & Edward Weston: A Passionate Collaboration.* Ms. Mather would have been astounded not only that there was a museum retrospective, or that she had become a heroine to feminist photographers worldwide, but that her name came first in the title before Weston's. This was something unthinkable 100 years earlier when she was part of the pioneering first wave of bohemian artists and feminists to settle in Los Angeles.

Weston's *Daybooks* are his journals that constitute the largest and most comprehensive diary of a photographer ever published; these books have only two missing sections (that we know of) which Weston tried to destroy, his time period in Los Angeles with Mather and his recollections of Tina Modotti upon hearing the news of her death in 1942. Clearly the journals from those times had something that was either embarrassing or that contradicted the myth of "Edward Weston" that had developed into a minor cult within the photographic world by 1960 when the *Daybooks* were published in separate volumes.

The *Daybooks* officially begin in August of 1923 with a planned journey by Weston and his young Italian assistant Tina de Richey to Mexico to explore this new post-revolutionary world. Clearly for Weston, in this second meeting of the minds with a female photographer, the tables had turned in his favor and it would now be Weston who was the master and Modotti who would be the naïve apprentice. But as we will see this is not a situation that would last for very long.

Hollywood

Modotti was not happy in Hollywood despite the fact that she was finally financially independent and was renting a large house that was always full of friends and eccentric hangers-on – most importantly her brief foray into cinema provided her with roles in three features in remarkably short order: *The Tiger's Coat* (1920), *Riding With Death* (1921) and *I Can Explain* (1922). By coincidence she played a Mexican in the latter two films as "Latin exoticism" was in vogue with Ramón Novarro, Dolores del Río and Lupe Vélez all well paid stars of the period playing "Mexicans" or "Latin" lovers.

Modotti, with her expressive face, dark eyes, broad forehead, sensual mouth and rich black hair would typically play the exotic vamp or the femme fatale. Her acting style, as captured on film, is theatrical, as was then the norm, but also emotionally powerful – she had very expressive hands and knew how to use them. Tina's face was able to convey a series of clearly defined emotions, beautifully using her eyes to direct attention and shifting expressions on cue with a power that was clearly under her complete control. One could see that she might have had a future in the film industry if she had wanted it, at least as long as the vogue for "Mexican" and "Latin" lovers lasted. That fascination peaked with Rudolph Valentino but by the sound era was finished – supplanted by homegrown stars such as Jimmy Stewart, Katharine Hepburn, Clark Gable and Carole Lombard, who were all American to the core. Even if Modotti had stayed in Hollywood it is doubtful that her career would have survived into the sound era. Still, many pretty actresses went to Hollywood and never got anywhere so by any stretch Modotti was a success with three pictures in three years. Nevertheless, she found the roles simplistic and would openly laugh at them, though they paid far better than modeling and she was now supporting two people.

Her contact with the Hollywood A-list seems to have been limited as she preferred to spend her time at home. There were also the bohemian soirees that often happened on weekends in Bunker Hill where the more adventurous film people mixed with writers and artists although most of those under contract by the studios in Hollywood went to fashionable restaurants such as the Formosa Café, which was also a speakeasy after-hours. While there is no record that she met any Hollywood royalty in some ways this is a shame as it would be interesting to know what she thought of Rudolph Valentino (a fellow immigrant from Italy), Louise Brooks, Charlie Chaplin, Anna May Wong, Josef Von Sternberg and Anita Loos, among others, who frequented both the fancy supper parties at the Hearst Mansion north of Los Angeles and the bohemian soirees on Bunker Hill where wine mixed freely with studio gossip and radical politics.

Modotti and Weston met in 1920 but had been in intersecting circles since 1918 so a meeting was almost certain at some point. They both knew the dancer Ramiel McGehee and the British poet John Cowper Powys. Modotti and Robo threw parties regularly in their large house, paid for by Tina's Hollywood career. When they finally did meet it was clear there was an attraction. Tina was attracted immediately to Weston's clear grasp of his art, his intelligence that seemed so nicely integrated into his sensitivity, his unselfconscious virility and sense of calm and control; meanwhile Weston was attracted to her extraordinary physical beauty, honest, expressive face and extreme, almost painful, sensitivity, as if she were living always on the edge, in the open – everything was on the surface, direct and unfiltered.

In 1921 Modotti started to pose for Weston in his Glendale studio but she posed for at least four other artists that we know of. It is here that they became lovers despite Weston's marriage and four children. Weston was in the habit of seducing his models, or trying to, on a regular basis and had casual girlfriends spread over the city. Modotti wrote him long amorous letters – then a norm for couples. He wrote to a friend, the photographer Johan Hagemeyer who lived in San Francisco: "I not only have done some of the best things yet – but also have had an exquisite affair...the pictures I believe to be especially good are of one Tina de Richey – a lovely Italian girl."[20]

Clearly Weston took a more worldly view of his "exquisite affair." We know from his letters that Modotti's husband Robo was aware her relationship with Weston but took it with an equal sense of fatalism and equanimity – incredibly it did not seem to affect his growing friendship with Weston. But Robo was aware that his marriage was in trouble and that Tina had many admirers. He may well have reasoned that a move to a new city might provide a re-start for his relationship.

Mexico City seemed promising for a variety of reasons and suddenly the possibility opened up – the minister of Public Education's Department of Fine Arts was José Vasconcelos, who had been impressed by Robo's batik designs and offered him a teaching position; and one of his best friends in Los Angeles, Ricardo Gómez Robelo, originally from Mexico City, had returned to take advantage of the expanding opportunities that seemed readily available. He offered the couple his house in the city and Robo immediately took the offer, but Tina hedged her bets and decided to stay, continuing to see Weston as his model, photographic apprentice and lover.

What kind of a place was Mexico City then after the revolution – what made it so attractive, not only to Weston and Modotti but to a whole cadre of intellectuals, artists, writers and their friends and lovers? One could make a case that Mexico City, along with Berlin and Paris, were the destinations of choice for this artistic, bohemian crowd after 1920, the date that the Revolution officially ended. While Berlin's Weimar period and Paris in the Twenties are very well-known and documented – even stamped with a zeitgeist that has become something of a cliché over the years – Mexico City remains something of an enigma where we see intersecting but conflicting trajectories that at a certain point seem to evaporate into smoke and mirrors. What was Mexico like in this period that has come to be known historically as "The Mexican Renaissance"?

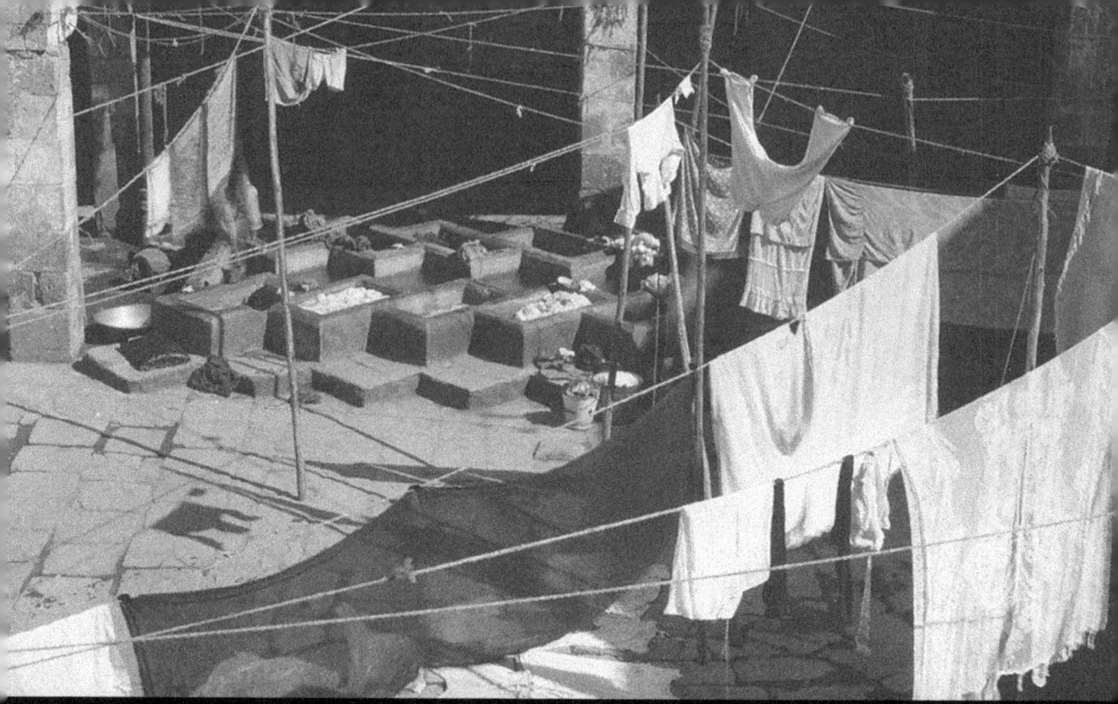

In Mexican mood the messiah is always accompanied by disaster: an earthquake, a conquest, a revolution, the sacrifice of a ruler; death and pain.

Anita Brenner, *Idols Behind Altars*

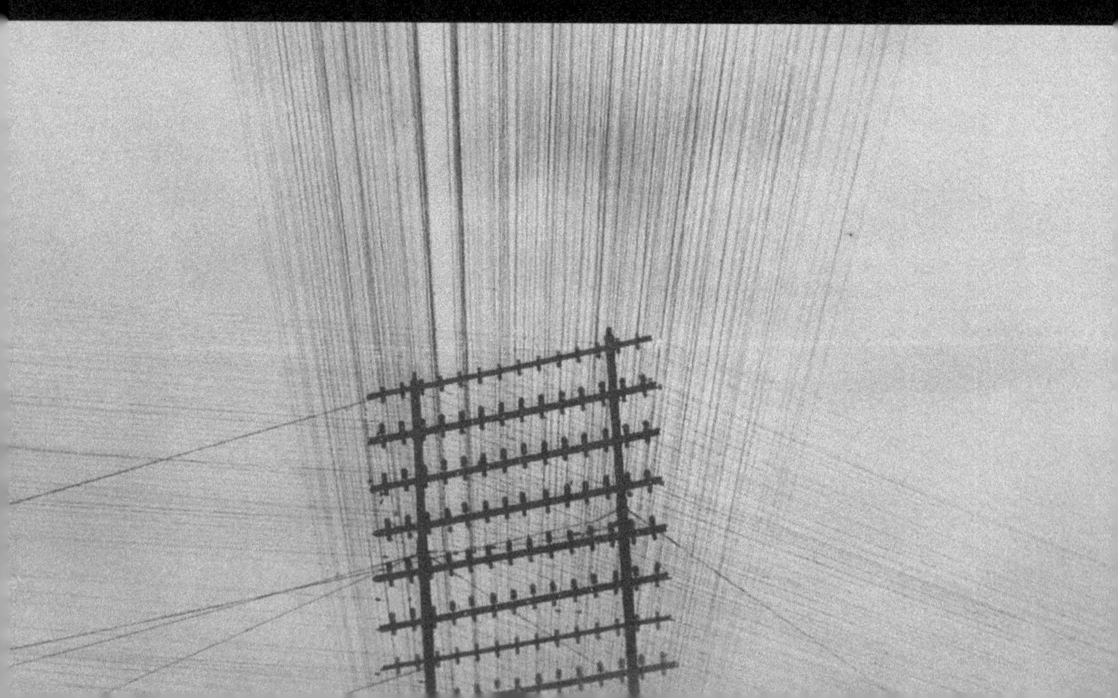

03

A Revolution and a Renaissance

Before we arrive at this Renaissance it would be useful to see the time before then to understand how such a profoundly conservative, Catholic country could produce the radical culture of the Twenties. First it is helpful to see the Mexican Revolution not as one single event – as it is often depicted in films of the period with swashbuckling Pancho Villa at the head of a ragtag army. The Revolution was actually an extended sequence of revolutions, counter-revolutions, coups d'état and aborted coups d'état – events that stretch out from 1910 to 1920.

The Revolution itself would probably not have happened without the massive financial devastation, political instability, and deep resentments that were all caused by the Mexican-American War (1846-1848). That war exposed the inability of the Mexican government to protect the people from invasion – for the Mexicans especially this was a sore point. First it was the Aztec civilization that had failed to protect them against the Spanish, then it was the democracy of President Antonio López de Santa Anna who failed to protect them against the Americans, surrendering to them in 1848. To the Mexican government it seemed that the way out of this morass, poverty and military weakness was through massive industrialization – it was a matter of "catching up" to the Americans and the Europeans – therefore vast swaths of land, owned by Mexican farmers and peasants, passed hands to large industries and railroad companies – ironically many of these companies were American and European. What came to be known as the Porfirian Land Law resulted in massive accumulation of wealth for the elite while displacing rural traditions and populations, spurring discontent and contempt for a government that had sold them out. The economic disparities, already at the breaking point, grew larger and more unstable. A Revolution seemed inevitable – it wasn't a question of if but when.

Meanwhile the American entrepreneur William Randolph Hearst, who owned a publishing empire, was stoking the fires of war, doing his best to push the US into the Mexican Revolution so he could cover it with his reporters and photographers already stationed in Mexico. Hearst had his team ready, all he needed was an actual war, but President Wilson was hedging his bets (a Wilson trademark). Hearst already had experience in "manufacturing consent" with the Spanish-American War (1898) where he learned to sensationalize news from Cuba to inflame American public opinion in favor of war with Spain. The only winners in such a war were, of course, the American oligarchs who saw in Cuba a vast source of wealth in the fruit, sugar and coffee plantations, beachfront real estate opportunities, and slave labor. In one famous case Hearst sent the mainstream Western artist Frederic Remington to Cuba in the Spring of 1897 to sketch "atrocities" for his publication and stoke the fires of war. Unfortunately, Remington cabled Hearst: "Everything is quiet. There is no trouble here. There will be no war – I wish to return." Hearst replied: "Please remain. You furnish the pictures and I'll furnish the war."[21] Despite some problems that war was seen as a success and Hearst used the more sophisticated methods available in the early century – particularly the newsreel – to full advantage in the next war in Mexico.

The Hearst papers even utilized fictionalized and dramatized newsreel accounts in order to sway American public opinion in support of military action. The fake newsreel was not invented by Hearst's team but already existed in Europe in the early 20th century, particularly France, and were called "actuality films." While actuality films – usually lasting one to three minutes – were meant to be documentaries they also made use of "event reconstructions." These reconstructions were filmed as real treating the documentary form as a style; for example, the shot of an actor playing a head of state might be partially obstructed by a hat, or an actress playing a famous royal arriving by car might be seen from the second story across the street. Some actuality films were shot before the news event took place and then released at the moment the event happened to maximize audience interest. Unfortunately, actuality films, like newspapers, were considered disposable – certainly they were not considered art in any sense as it was understood then – and were almost all discarded once the depicted event passed.

Hearst's main man in Mexico City was William Selig, a Hollywood pioneer who specialized in newsreels, that by then ran to 10 minutes, and was head of a profitable cinematic tabloid of popular and news events that told the news in easily digestible narratives – a format still in place today. Hearst's primary motive in his push to war was his radical belief in American exceptionalism; he saw the smart use of hard and soft power in the Caribbean and South America as essential to American interests. President Theodore Roosevelt agreed, tweaking the Monroe Doctrine in 1904 with a "Roosevelt Corollary," thereby asserting the US's right to intervene in Latin American nations to maintain "stability," effectively making the US an "international police force" in the Western Hemisphere. The fact that another fake war, as in Cuba, needed to be staged in Mexico – alongside a real revolution – for the American press to have conflict, "drama," and public entertainment is surely a harbinger of things to come.

Woodrow Wilson, the American president, after some prodding (and much in need of the Hearst's papers approval), provided the war, sending 5,000 troops into what came to be called the Pershing Expedition into Chihuahua, Mexico, in 1916. Hearst's interests in Mexico were not only political but personal and financial. He owned a one-million-acre ranch in Chihuahua named Babicora where he raised cattle.[22] Carranza eventually forced the US to withdraw in 1917 when the US, and Hearst's newspapers, became busy in another war in Europe that seemed more urgent and more promising.

The crooked and corrupt president who was overthrown that started the ball rolling was Porfirio Díaz. While unpopular to almost everyone, regardless of their politics, no one suspected in 1910 that the aging Díaz was about to become a prelude to the "defining event of modern Mexican history."[23] To make matters worse Díaz knew he was unpopular and promised to step down, but then his backers encouraged him to seek reelection so he reneged on his promise. With labor unrest high, land distribution being debated in the streets, strikes a regular feature of life, the polarization was extreme and sometimes violent. When wealthy landowner Francisco Madero challenged Díaz in a bid to "restore order" Díaz jailed him. Madero in turn called for a general armed uprising against Díaz and fled temporarily to the US to regroup.

Rebellions broke out all over Mexico and seemed to ignite the country like kindling ready for a match – as if Madero's call to revolution had sparked not only his own right-wing call to "law and order" but revolutions from various factions at once – far beyond the control of one man. Madero won the local battle but immediately faced the armed rebellion of Emiliano Zapata, a rebel fighting for land reform, and Victoriano Huerta, Madero's right-hand man entrusted to control Mexico City. Huerta staged a successful coup d'état backed by the Americans who saw Huerta as a fool but also a useful "strongman." Predictably Madero was assassinated as he was being escorted to prison with his family and Huerta moved to consolidate power.

In a touch of the absurd the ultra-rightist Huerta's accession to power accomplished the impossible: all of the warring leftist factions united briefly and overthrew Huerta in 16 months despite the fact that he was backed by US business interests, ultra-rightist factions and the Catholic Church. Taft the American president viewed Huerta as good for business interests and so supported him but never took Huerta seriously as a leader, while Wilson the succeeding president was even less enthusiastic.

The subsequent alliance of Pancho Villa and Emiliano Zapata during the Revolution, based around a peasant revolt and land reform, would put any Mexican soap opera to shame. The Americans feared both Villa and Zapata seeing them as unstable, committed radicals unlikely to become good business partners even if, temporarily, they played by Washington's tune. The Americans put their chips with Carranza sensing a good, long-term trading partner.

In 1917 the Mexican government under Carranza created a new constitution but many of the factions that took part -Villanistas and Zapatistas in particular – wanted a radical constitution not to Carranza's liking, but as the historian Frank McLynn put it, "the constitution was drawn up by the soldiers of the Revolution, not the politicians or the lawyers."[24] In a familiar move Carranza ordered the execution of Zapata, the odd man out, but the radical Constitution passed anyway even without Zapata's help.

Álvaro Obregón came to power with overwhelming popular support in 1920 and things settled down but there is no consensus as to when the Revolution ended as the factions continued fighting not only in the press but sometimes on the streets with insurrections and assassinations springing up occasionally, becoming part of the everyday life of Mexico City. The Revolution was a disaster both financially and for the everyday life of Mexican families. Statistics are sketchy but estimates range from 1 million to as high as 2.7 million people killed (1910–1920), many of them noncombatants, women and children who were in the wrong place at the wrong time.

From the American perspective Obregón was a good choice to consolidate warring factions as he lacked his own political agenda except to stay alive, get rich, and remain in power. He handed the right their victories by appeasing the US in mining and industry and he handed the left their victory by keeping the radical Constitution intact. Everyone grumbled but not too loudly. What made Obregón so important for artists, intellectuals and writers was that this radical constitution was not simply an abstract piece of paper but a blueprint for a new society that was quickly taken from the drawing board to the street. A brief window opened up and let in some badly needed oxygen – it didn't last for very long but it was crucially important for the Mexican Renaissance.

Obregón chose José Vasconcelos to run the cultural programs, a man who modeled himself on the Soviet Union's cultural czar Anatoly Lunacharsky.[25] Both Ministers were fundamentally radical left populists who spent money on education reform, well-trained teachers, educational programs for the poor, and new museums and subsidized publishing ventures for artists, writers, and graphic designers – all paid for by taxing the rich and new investment coming into Mexico now that the Revolution was history.

Vasconcelos used his position to make the Ministry of Education a cultural and educational "patron" for artists, muralists, graphic designers, writers, and academic intellectuals from all walks of life. There was, as to be expected, a steady stream of Latin American cultural producers in the vanguard, including activists and hangers-on, that quickly rushed to Mexico City to see what was happening and look for work – many down-and-out bohemian artists/writers from New York to Santiago made the trek to Mexico City. Even successful Mexican artists who were in exile – most famously Diego Rivera – also returned triumphantly to brass bands and speeches.

Intellectuals from South America also found a home in Mexico City, most famously the Chilean poet Gabriela Mistral, who arrived in 1923. The Nicaraguan writer Salómon de la Selva also settled in the city eventually becoming more involved in radical politics that eventually got him into trouble. Peruvian intellectuals also settled in the city, including the famous Marxist theoretician José Carlos Mariátegui, along with Magda Portal, a political feminist activist within APRA, a Peruvian hybrid version of socialism/communism. From Cuba the best-known immigrant revolutionary was Julio Antonio Mella who fled Cuba in 1926 and settled in Mexico City where he built up a network of political refugees – Mella would become important to Modotti's life later after Weston had returned to California.

After 1920 the revolutionary diaspora gathered in Mexico City – then with a population of slightly over 1 million people – mirrored its artists, writers and even art historians (Anita Brenner). These people were part of an expanding transnational network of radical activists and insurgent artists, poets and academics, who all, despite their differences and countries of origin, practiced a mobile form of contentious politics. Many of these people were young and full of revolutionary adventure – they were peripatetic and enthusiastic for radical ideas whatever their country of provenance. The discussed their ideas – Marxist, socialist, anarchist and libertarian – and disseminated their manifestos through articles, pamphlets and public meetings – their ongoing push to create a new world constitutes what Argentinian scholar Martin Bergel called "a militant traveling culture."[26] This is the world that seemed appealing to Weston and Modotti and why they took a chance and boarded a train from Los Angeles to Mexico. Weston returned after three years and never set foot in the country again; Modotti never returned to the US and never looked back – her life would be irrevocably changed.

Edward Weston: *Tina, Los Angeles*

By the time Weston made *The White Iris, 1921* in his studio in Glendale, using Modotti as his model, he was still deploying the soft-focus peculiar to Pictorialism while shifting to a more formalist arrangement of his frame. The iris and Modotti's head create an arc that meets at the top of the image and her nipple is at the extreme bottom, not only turning the portrait into a nude but daringly leaving the center of the image in total darkness – something he had learned from Mather but now made his own by fusing it with his own romantic version of formalism.

With *Tina, Los Angeles, 1921* Weston photographs Modotti wearing a heavy winter coat as she brings those expressive hands up to cover her neck in an incredible gesture of vulnerability – it's one of his great shots and Modotti here is a full partner. The image reminds one of Marlene Dietrich's highly dramatic, almost operatic, collaborations in Hollywood with the eccentric maestro Josef von Sternberg.

With the daring and unconventional *Tina Modotti With Arms Raised, 1921* Weston moves to a sharper-edged focus and a more monumental blocking. He places Modotti, without makeup, at the center, eyes closed, with her arms up like an early Greek kore. But unlike these archaic sculptures the face looks completely modern as Tina appears to be in transition from one gesture to another, her lips full, about to speak. It's the most modernist image in Weston's body of work up to that point. The photograph is indebted to Stieglitz's influential *Georgia O'Keeffe* (1918) where the sharply detailed photo cuts off the top of O'Keeffe's head giving primary importance to her hands and eyes. With *Tina Modotti Arms Raised* Weston follows that lead but takes it a step further – he has forgone the artistic pose as Modotti simply raises her arms up in a fully frontal, direct and daring confrontation with the camera. It's a portrait that goes much further into modernism's brutalist vocabulary – outside the scope of either Mather or Stieglitz.

The Los Angeles-based Weston had caught up with the New York avant-garde. He knew that *Tina, Los Angeles, 1921* and *Tina Modotti With Arms Raised* were now as good or better than anything Stieglitz, or anyone else, was doing. The logical thing to do here was to consolidate his new gains, organize his new work into a portfolio and take it to New York. He had the connections and the time – but he didn't do that. He decided to gamble. It was time to take his photography elsewhere, very far from the salons, the museums and the photo shows – and also far from his wife and kids. Now was Weston's chance and he took it.

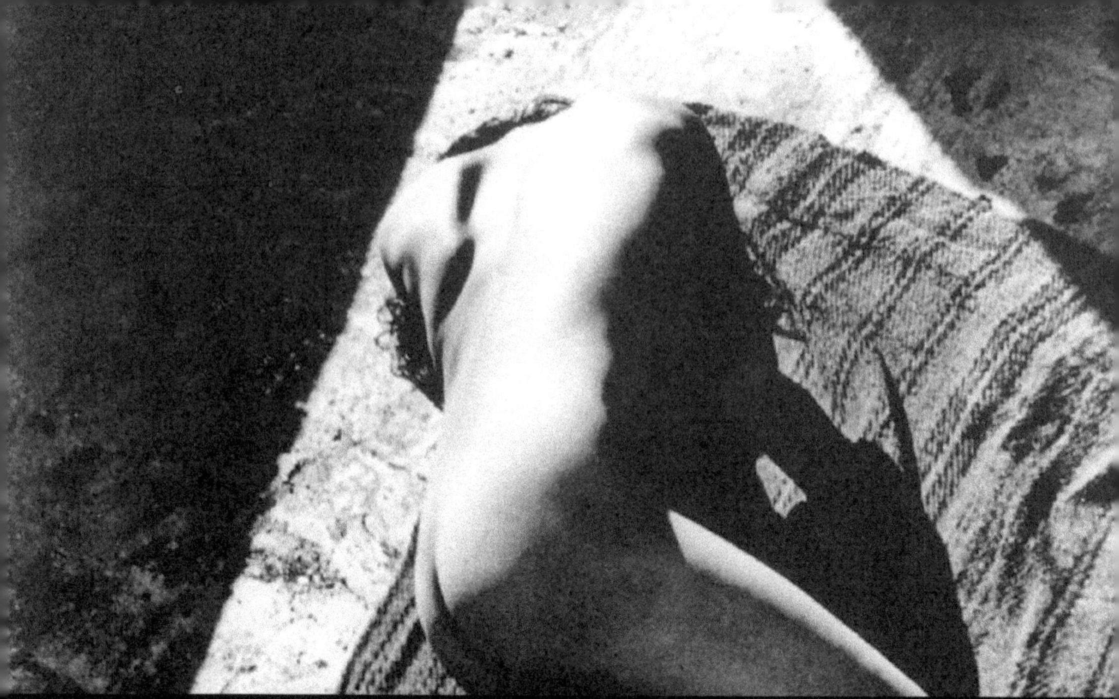

Love is the revelation of the other person's freedom.

Octavio Paz

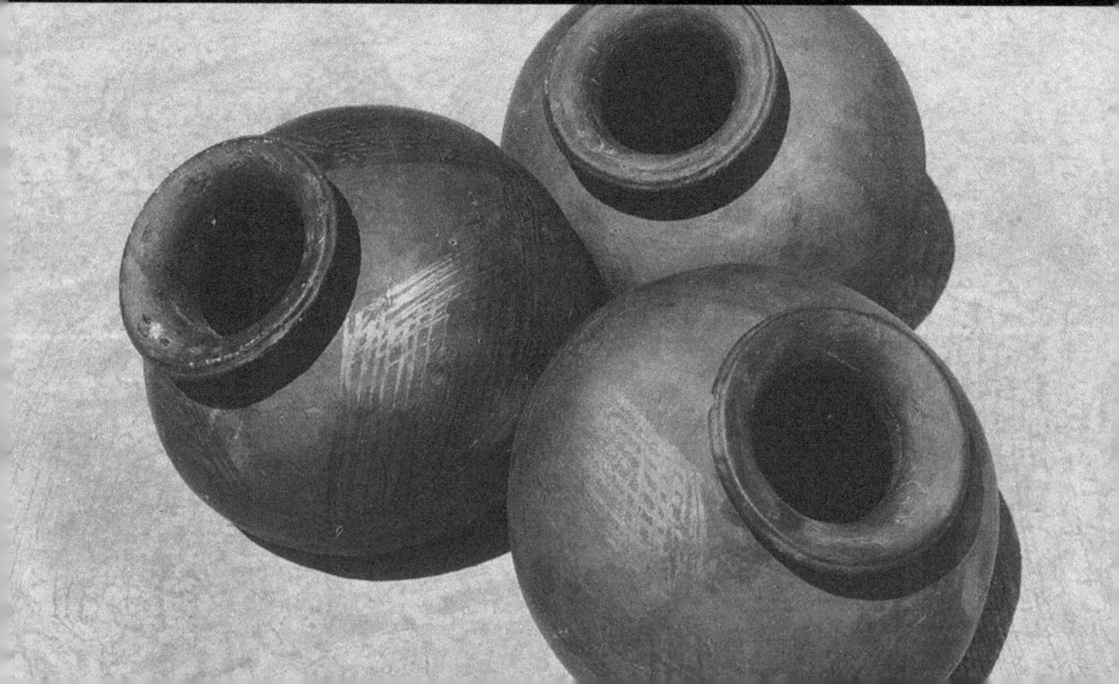

04

Aztec Land

Mexican Folkways

Robo left for Mexico City in December of 1921 taking his batiks, photographs by Weston and Mather, along with work by other Los Angeles-based artists, hoping to mount an exhibition of their work. At that point a new kind of society and mindset started to appear even among people who were not intellectuals and not directly involved in the literary or artistic avant-garde, and it was possible to get an audience for a new kind of work. This is Patricia Albers:

> Robo had arrived in Mexico as the revolution's end was unleashing vast energies and firing the people's will to cure their society's ills and forge a new destiny. In July 1921 the reform-minded strongman President Alvaro Obregón appointed an ingenious and hardworking Oaxacan lawyer and philosopher named José Vasconcelos to the key position of minister of public education. Underpinning the program was his concept of Mexico's vanguard "cosmic race," a people of mixed blood, Indian in soul, and Spanish in language and civilization. By the end of 1921 a wealth of experiments were in progress. Cheap editions of the classics were flying off government presses to be distributed to the people. Free workshops and concerts abounded, public libraries opened their doors...Ricardo Robelo's position at the right hand of Vasconcelos, a childhood friend, put him at the center of the capital's artistic and cultural effervescence.[27]

Robo, who was Robelo's houseguest in the city, would be able to take full advantage of the new opportunities opening up all around him. It seemed like the fresh start he had always sought was finally within reach.

Aside from writing constant letters to Tina, Robo wrote to Weston, encouraging him to also come to Mexico City, calling it an "artist's paradise" and suggesting they share a studio in the city.[28] His excitement is palpable in his prose: "There is more poetry in one lone serape shrouded figure leaning in the door of a pulque

[sp] shot at twilight or a bronzen [sp] daughter of the Aztecs nursing her child in the church than can be found in Los Angeles in ten years."[29] After putting off the trip so often their friends in Los Angeles started to tease them about it, Modotti and Weston decided to go to Mexico separately and discreetly. Finally on February 3 Tina took the train to El Paso to make the connection to Mexico City. On the trip she received the news that Robo had contracted smallpox and urged her to turn back. Modotti refused and one day later she finally got into Mexico City, greeted by Ricardo Robelo, the owner of the house where Robo lived during his two months in Mexico.

By the time she arrived Robo was dead. Predictably in one of his last letters to Weston, full of doubts and procrastinations, Robo had written that the planned exhibition was stalled and not going anywhere: "Perhaps she [Tina] can get this exhibit started – I cannot."[30] Tina did just that, surprising even herself by finding she had a talent for organizing and getting people to work on a deadline. Aside from Weston and Robo, the show included paintings by Nell Blane, a watercolor artist best known for her bright colored, loosely brushed style, along with photographs by Margrethe Mather, Arnold Schröder and Jane Reece. She settled the exhibition dates with the Academy of Fine Arts under Robelo who tutored Modotti in the practical aspects of installation. He also seems to have fallen under her spell, becoming a suffering and devoted admirer.

Tina staffed the gallery, greeting visitors, explaining the artworks and giving biographical details. While the exhibition was a great success some visitors seemed to do a double take seeing the sweet, soft-spoken widow dressed in black greeting them at the door and the sultry naked beauty depicted by Weston on the walls – was it possible they were the same person? Modotti put off the question while it went begging. The myth of Tina as the mysterious, exotic femme fatale was beginning to form under her watch.

Modotti was at a crossroads. Her father died only a few months after her husband and as she traveled to San Francisco for the funeral by train she considered opening a photographic studio there, like her uncle, but it came to nothing. She self-published a book on Robo's work, his poetry and batiks, titled *The Book of Robo,* that was in a sense a parting gift. Weston, with the success of the group exhibit in Mexico, had finally decided to make the trip south. In November 1922 Weston and Modotti resumed their intimacy and made plans to move together and establish a portrait studio in Mexico City. They established a simple oral contract; Weston would teach Modotti all aspects of photography that she didn't already know, especially the difficult darkroom work where

Weston was an acknowledged master. Because of her language and social skills she would run the business end of their studio and portrait business, as well as run the house.

They had a maid/cook, Elisa, who would become part of their family in the three years they were together. Flora Chandler would generously send money regularly to cover costs not met by what they earned from their photography. They did not discuss the personal details, the sexual aspect, of this "contract" but they clearly imagined being free to do as they saw fit and follow their instincts, their desires, to wherever they might lead – this "open relationship" was undoubtedly part of the adventure. Flora Chandler and her sons drove out to San Pedro harbor in Los Angeles to see Weston, their eldest son, then 13 years old, and Modotti off on their expedition in July 1923.

This is Margaret Hooks on their arrival in Mexico:

> First impressions are always important and Tina and Edward's were favorable. The hated middle-class morality of the United States was now behind them and they made no concessions to it. They used their own names, refusing to pose as a married couple, and no one in hotels or elsewhere questioned why Tina Modotti and Edward Weston were living together or sharing a room. The dreaded Ku Klux Klan would not bother them here.[31]

The Klan were notorious not only as racists who often resorted to vigilante violence, but also for privately enforcing miscegenation laws that enforced racial segregation at the level of marriage or intimate relations between members of different races. While law enforcement officials often looked the other way Klan members did not and often took matters into their own hands. With the recent sedition laws passed by President Wilson that made it a federal crime to criticize the government (landing Eugene Debs the socialist/pacifist candidate for president in jail) and the prohibition laws that made alcohol illegal, one understands why a wide swath of American intellectuals and artists moved to Europe and Mexico.

Weston and Modotti were fascinated by *pulquerias,* bars that specialized in the traditional brew, *pulque*. This is a distilled maguey-cactus mash that is sometimes mixed with fruit juice to soften its high alcohol content. Traditionally *pulquerias* had brightly colored murals that adorned their fronts that were thematically linked to the colorful names that Modotti and Weston noted, although they didn't photograph them for some time fearing that they might fall into the trap of photographing the cliché "picturesque Mexico."[32] This became a strategy that they consistently stuck to, and much impressed other photographers. That is, they would go to a site and scout it out for ways to shoot it, discuss the best place for camera set-ups, and the best time of day suited for shooting, then return later at another date with camera equipment.

When they finally decided to photograph *pulquerias* it was as an assignment paid for by *Mexican Folkways,* the popular magazine edited by Tina's friend, the anthropologist Frances Toor who had come to Mexico City to experience the Mexican Renaissance for herself. They photographed the *pulquerias* side by side in the summer of 1926, using a formalist approach that undercut the "picturesque Mexico" aspects they sought to nullify. One senses from this agreement to first avoid the picturesque and then to find a photographic solution to it that they were thinking together as a unit. Weston's *Pulqueria* (1926) and Modotti's *Exterior de Pulqueria* (1926) use frontal placement with the edges of the bar square with the picture plane, with the human element barely visible and cut off at the bottom. The *Pulqueria* series would be the first project that caught their imagination as they entered Mexico and the last project they would complete together, shooting side by side.

This is Patricia Albers:

> From the moment of her arrival, Tina was claimed by Mexico, whose spirit resonated with childhood memories...Responding to her impressions of a vaguely Italianate culture, Tina professed to "feel Mexican when I am in Mexico, unlike the United States where I feel I am in a foreign country." Indeed many mistook her for a compatriot "until I open my mouth," she said laughing, and out tumbled charmingly botched Spanish colored by an Italian lilt and a North American accent.[33]

Even Weston felt at home in Mexico and when he returned briefly to Los Angeles to visit his family he wrote in his journal: "I walked the streets of Los Angeles and found myself a stranger – a foreigner. Who were all of these drab gray people? Not my kind!"[34]

Weston and Modotti visited and befriended Diego Rivera at the Ministry of Public Education where the artist, only recently returned from exile in Paris, was working on his mural at the ministry with a handful of assistants and admirers. Rivera had shifted radically from Cubist small-scale work that he had been doing – to great success in Paris – to monumental realist allegories that used some of the visual vocabulary of Cubism but in a completely different context, incorporating traditional Mexican folk art and Italian fresco motifs in grand visual symphonies – all paid for by the new government.

Rivera would eventually hire Modotti to shoot his murals as they were difficult to photograph due to the lighting conditions. When he saw the results Jose Clemente Orozco also hired her. Modotti was so successful that she turned the project into a lifelong profession, that is, photographing the work of other artists. When Rivera sent prints to MoMA in New York so the curators there could see photographs of his work the prints were by Modotti, but it is unlikely that the curators were aware of who she was or that the prints they held were themselves works of art.

Later Tina would also become a model for Rivera for his mural *The Abundant Earth* at the National Agricultural School in Chapingo, a small town located about 25 km northeast of Mexico City. Rivera used one of Weston's shots, *Tina on the Azotea* (1924), as inspiration but Modotti also posed for him. Rivera worked on the ambitious series of murals between 1926 and 1927. It was then that Modotti entered into an affair with Rivera that lasted about a year and was noted by his then wife Lupe Marín, who eventually divorced the womanizing Rivera who had many simultaneous lovers of different ages, nationalities and physical characteristics. The only person who could possibly keep up with him was the sybaritic Frida Kahlo, whom he married in 1929. Modotti had no illusions about Rivera and the separation after the mural project was finished was amicable.

Despite Weston's own constant short-term affairs Modotti's lifestyle caused a rift between them that never healed. Margaret Hooks: "Professionally, Tina and Edward were getting along well, but their love relationship was unsteady and their feelings towards each other fluctuated dramatically. Despite occasional passionate encounters, they maintained quite separate lives."[35] Brett Weston, then 13 years old, many years after the fact remembered finding Tina and his father together. Having forgotten the key to the house he had to climb the iron-grille work of the door to the balcony and found Edward pouring oil over Tina naked in bed. Weston said they found it disconcerting to see his son out in the balcony and no doubt it was something of a trauma for Brett as well since he remembered it vividly 60 years later.[36]

Modotti was determined not to become simply Weston's appendage, nor to be seen as just his mistress. "Edward was spending many hours alone and complaining at length of Tina's numerous admirers and suitors. There appears to have been a fundamental problem regarding the understanding they had reached in Los Angeles."[37] Weston didn't speak the language so stayed mostly at home while Modotti was a social being and spoke the language more fluently by the day – they led very different lives and that gap would only widen over time. In the meantime their house was the place to be in Mexico City. Even Rivera and Lupe Marín would host parties at "Edward and Tina's" house rather than their own because it was better suited for dancing – then a standard activity at parties – and Modotti had traditional Saturday night fiestas. Here Margaret Hooks describes a typical evening:

> There was little attempt at serious discussion – it was the "art" of having a good time that mattered. Eating, drinking, singing and dancing lasted all night, occasionally deteriorating into pistol shots at dawn as party guests became overexcited. A lively and vivacious Tina was at the center of it all, sometimes serving up Italian spaghetti and red wine, always the focus of the male guests' attention.[38]

There was always an incoming flux of new arrivals from various countries who had heard not only of the Mexican Renaissance but of the famous fiestas of "Edward and Tina" – in one evening Weston counted seven different nationalities present.

Weston, Brett and Modotti settled in their studio in the Colonia Juaréz section of D.F. not far from the city center. From its inaugural issue *Mexican Folkways,* a bilingual magazine for people interested in art, culture and art history, had featured advertising for the Weston/Modotti team. It read: "Photographs – Por traits – Edward Weston/Tina Modotti Av. Veracruz 42 – Tel. Ericsson, Condesa 38." Significantly both names were on the ad – their specialty was portraiture. The neighborhood then was full of young up-and-coming business-oriented families with disposable incomes – a clientele well suited to buying photographs. Nevertheless, when Weston left Mexico City three years later he destroyed all of his commercial work taking with him only his personal pictures so there would be no record of his commercial activities, as he intended.

My Latest Lover

During Diego Rivera's and Lupe Marín's early stages of marriage they lived in a collective arts workshop with several small independent houses that faced each other across a narrow alley in a commercial district. The tenants were all hard drinking, slow to pay their rent and bohemian, but the rowdiest and loudest were undoubtedly Diego and Lupe. It was here that Modotti, on one of her social calls, found a collection of Mexican marionettes tucked away underneath Rivera's Cubist paintings done in Paris. A local couple, Germán and Lola Cueto, had founded a marionette theater for which Germán sculpted all of the marionettes by hand while Lola did the stage design. Here Tina photographed a marionette whose dark costume melds into its own silhouette. Modotti has burned in the shadow so the marionette appears to be squaring off or dancing to its own shadow, or perhaps death itself – the picture has a dark edge despite the lighthearted subject.

The photograph's formalist credentials are also in full view as the marionette's sombrero and its own shadow bisect the image near the top at an angle while the open legs create a triangle near the bottom as if precariously balancing the mustachioed marionette – looking like Weston dressed up as a Mexican ranchero. Modotti was rightfully pleased with it and sent a copy to her friend Johan Hagemeyer – the title of the work was *My Latest Lover,* a satire of her own reputation. When Johan showed Weston the print he exclaimed: "Tina has taken a photograph that I wish I could sign with my name – that does not happen often in my life!"[39] For many photo art historians *My Latest Lover* is Modotti's first great serious work, containing within it all of the themes that would preoccupy her for the remainder of her short career.

Aztec Land Teahouse and Bookstore

Modotti also used her newfound knowledge of exhibition planning and installation by putting together the first Weston one-man show to run for two weeks starting in October 1922 at Aztec Land, a teahouse and bookstore that also sold handcrafted objets d'art, but in their mezzanine exhibited contemporary art, usually paintings. Modotti presided over the guest register during its hours of operation, and the first, typically enigmatic entry in the guest book was her own: "Long life to your work – the only thing which never fails you – Tina Modotti-R. Mexico, 1923."

On the invitation to the exhibit the pair displayed a quote by the Mexican art critic Marius de Zayas: "Photography begins to be photography for until now it has only been art."[40] The quote is a direct and very clear attack against Pictorialism and a support for the new photographic works then coming into prominence that were more socially conscious, or simply more formally focused on the medium itself. In any case Weston and Modotti had drawn the line in the sand.

The Aztec Land show was an enormous success with approximately 1,000 viewers passing through in a two-week period. Weston's work was a revelation to many artists, photographers and intellectuals as modernist photography had not gained a foothold in Mexico and many people were not aware that Pictorialist conventions had been overthrown, or that there was a revolution in photography happening in Europe where the new smaller cameras, most famously the Leica 35mm, were changing the medium forever. An even more radical revolution was happening in the USSR with younger artists, such as Alexander Rodchenko, who made use of the smaller format cameras to shoot urban views from unusual angles, using off-center framing that was consciously anticlassical. Thanks largely to Stieglitz and the 291 Gallery Weston was not only familiar with such pictures but had talked about them in New York with fellow artists who understood the new work and could discuss its advantages and drawbacks.

Weston was finally noticed and written about as an artist, something he had sought for years, thanks to the Aztec Land show. This is Rene d'Harnoncourt, the Viennese born curator who lived and worked in Mexico City in the 1920s and many years later ran MoMA in New York:

> To meet Edward Weston wandering through Mexico in the middle Twenties was a wonderful experience. Mexicans had just begun to explore their own country and the twentieth century and were busy transforming the things they liked best among their discoveries into a New World culture. Edward Weston felt the excitement of this process deeply...His work in turn was a revelation for the Mexican artists who previously had given photography little attention as an art form.[41]

Visitors to Aztec Land also came to look at the pictures of Tina Modotti that astounded people with their naturalism and erotic power. Such works had not been seen previously because in conventional photographic nudes, that were as old as the medium, photographers consistently referenced classical painting, presumably giving their pictures the imprimatur of high art – in effect, the images were "fine art signaling." The other sort of photographic nude was pornography where the objective was to show as much as possible of a naked woman or man using suggestive poses and props that were often meant to be amusing. Weston's work avoided all of these conventions, going in a different direction entirely.

The pictures concealed as much as they showed; they were erotic but also somewhat removed, cool, studied and formal; they were carefully framed, yet had the spontaneity of a snapshot; they were clearly portraits due to the importance accorded to the face but also nudes; moreover, there seemed to be a communication of sorts, a silent dialogue, happening between subject and photographer. The pictures seemed to incorporate a sense of montage and mise-en-scène within the single frame that suggested a cinema still, but a still that had managed to compact a whole film within it. How did Weston pull off these contradictions together within a single shot?

Photographers in particular were drawn to the exhibit and had many questions – the enthusiasm was palpable. For that short period in 1923 Aztec Land became the central focal point for photographic study in Mexico City. While the show only sold eight prints – six of them nudes – Weston and Modotti considered the show a success not only because of the large number of visitors but because of the intensity of their reactions – the word was out.

Aztec Land did regular group exhibitions that Weston participated in until he returned to the US in 1926. The following year, 1924, Weston did another one-person show and Tina again signed the guest book: "Tina Modotti – your apprentice of the past – present – and may she be of the future. Mexico, 1924." Weston was proud of his "dear apprentice" and noted that Modotti's prints "lose nothing in comparison with mine – they are her own expression."[42] Following the show Tina and Edward participated in a group show at the Palacio de Mineria along with their friends the painters Jean Charlot and Rafael Sala so exhibitions were now a regular routine factor in their lives.

For the Aztec Land show of 1924 the writer Francisco Garcia Icazbalceta wrote a glowing review of the exhibition where Weston first showed his pyramid photographs as well the nude photos of Tina on the *azotea*. This is Garcia Icazbalceta: "With *Tina with Kimono* (1924) Modotti covers her body with a kimono displaying her nude torso, a close shot that brought out the detail, therefore form and space; or the magnifying lens, if not the microscope, the partial vision."[43] Garcia notes that, contrary to custom, Weston has fragmented the nude. While today such fragmentation is commonplace it was customary in nude photography to show the whole body and imply some form of "classical" or "painterly" artistic formal effects – Weston bluntly avoids these conventions. In Garcia's comments on the *Piramide del Sol* (1924) he smartly suggests that the sloping pre-Hispanic staircase pyramid offers "an image related to semiabstract cubism."[44]

A great deal of Modotti's fame, or notoriety, after the Aztec Land exhibit was due to those *azotea* pictures but: "Tina had no intention of being a mere ornament. She gave rebirth to herself not only as "Mexican" but also as a photographer of Mexico. A state of creativity was summoned up and sustained in her, to wither not long after she left the country. In an emotionally expansive mood, she set about making pictures."[45] But Modotti always had her own beauty to contend with – a dangerous double-edged sword that was difficult to control. She was, even in culturally elite circles, sometimes derisively referred to as "the *It* girl of the avant-garde." For Clara Bow, a famous and wealthy Hollywood actress and flapper, that "*It*" was a term of approbation, even awe – Bow's film *It* (1927) created the term and set the pace. But in the case of Modotti "*It*" was meant as a slight, a sarcastic epithet – a slap so she should know her place.

Trying Too Hard to Be Avant-garde

In the studio Modotti enjoyed toying with modernist techniques such as reverse printing or cutting the paper in off angles to create unusual abstractions, using the darkroom as a laboratory to create one-of-a-kind works. Weston didn't generally like these modernist techniques (nor did Stieglitz) finding them affected and "trying too hard to be avant-garde." Weston felt instinctively that he could recognize and see the difference between great avant-garde work and bullshit. Modotti's abstractions also came to resemble in many cases abstract paintings, in effect returning to the problem encountered with Pictorialism, where painting is the benchmark. As Paul Strand put it, one had to let go of the "training wheels of art" (his term) and look only to the medium of photography itself.

At one point Weston compared Modotti's more radical pictures, which unfortunately have not survived, to Man Ray's work, finding hers to be better.[46] This clearly shows that by this point they were both familiar with the European avant-garde. Although Man Ray was actually from Philadelphia, in the Northeast US, by the time of his entry into modernist photography with solarization, reverse printing, Rayograms, as well as his iconic pictures of his muse Lee Miller, he was a seasoned Parisian. Likewise, Modotti, despite her impoverished background, was self-taught in the arts and by the 1920s was well versed in literature, philosophy, modernist music and art that she instinctively gravitated to while Weston was cautious, critical and often dismissive.

Tina Modoti and Frida Kahlo

In one of their evening get-togethers, or *tertulias,* with Tina's circle, that included Weston, Rivera and his wife Lupe, Modotti struck up a friendship with a short (even shorter than herself) funky, smart-ass, wisecracking, prankish 16-year-old named Frida Kahlo. Patricia Albers: "Frida quickly fell under Tina's sway, joining the Party and shedding her schoolgirl blouses and baubles for the workmanlike shirts and A-line skirts that Tina deemed proper for a Communist."[47] Kahlo also joined "Los Cachucas," a Marxist group at the National Preparatory School, and later the Young Communist League. For a time, Frida's only adornment was an enameled hammer-and-sickle pin, a gift from Tina.

Patricia Albers: "Even more momentous than her conversion to communism, however, was the young woman's encounter with Diego Rivera at one of the lively *tertulias* Tina still threw from time to time."[48] Rivera, who was married at the time, came into the party guns blazing (literally) shooting the record player simply because he felt like it. Kahlo – no stranger to eccentricity – took notice. Rivera was then already famous and working on his mural *The Creation* in the Bolivar Auditorium in the center of the city. Six years later Kahlo and Rivera started a more serious love affair that would culminate in their marriage in 1929.

Kahlo and Modotti had some things in common that would have made friendship likely. Kahlo's father Guillermo was a German-born photographer who taught her the basic mechanics of photography and darkroom work while Modotti had an uncle who was a professional photographer who ran his own studio – they understood the power of image making as a matter of course. Both women were openly defiant of bourgeois norms and social pressure to conform to the point of risking their professional standing as artists and even their personal safety. For example, when living legend (and powerful promoter) André Breton praised Kahlo's work she called him and his Surrealist friends "artistic bitches."[49] Surely the wrong thing to say if you want to impress but that was not Kahlo's (or Modotti's) style. Typically, Rivera and Modotti found it funny and, more importantly from our perspective, they thought it was just the right thing to say – this tells us a great deal about them and their camaraderie, their humor, and their style. They knew they were great artists, even if their lives were a mess, and didn't need the blessing or imprimatur of a French intellectual to tell them so. In any case Kahlo didn't agree with Breton's ideas about painting "dreams" (á la Salvador Dali) since she always insisted that she had no interest in dreams and painted only her "reality."

Kahlo and Modotti were rumored to have had a sexual affair as both women had open relationships with a variety of lovers but Kahlo was more openly bisexual and her love life was varied and dangerously complicated – the fact that she divorced and then remarried Diego Rivera is only a minor drama in the story of her convulsive life. Khalo's lovers also varied widely in age and sexual orientation, from the conservative (sexually speaking) Leon Trotsky to the cross-dressing, pistol packing, wild woman from Costa Rica, Chavela Vargas, they all fell under the spell of Kahlo's otherworldly charms. In any case there is no hard evidence of an affair between Modotti and Kahlo, only rumors in letters and writings of the period and essays and biographies written after the fact.

Strangely Modotti never photographed Kahlo and Kahlo never painted Modotti despite their deep friendship. While some photographs of Kahlo have been ascribed to Modotti on the web and social media they were more likely taken by Rivera or Nickolas Muray, a good professional photographer and another of Kahlo's lovers hoping to marry her after she divorced Diego, but it was not to be. There is a charming photo taken by Muray in 1928 of Kahlo and Modotti, arms round each other, legs crossed, hands on hips, in fashionable jazz age dresses outdoors in Mexico City. A double portrait of Muray and Frida with him charmingly stepping to the side behind her was probably a self-portrait. Muray sold pictures regularly to the lucrative American magazine market and was one of the few photographers, if not the only one, stationed in Mexico who actually made a good living from his work. Many of the stunning color photos from the Casa Azul are his. Rivera seems to have been bemused by Muray's infatuation with his wife, never taking him seriously as a challenge, either as an artist or as a companion to Frida.

Something else that Kahlo and Modotti had in common is that they both chose as partners men who were recognized masters in their field of art. They both had the advantage of having such a person present to bounce off ideas and the disadvantage of having to overcome being seen merely as "the wife" or "the mistress" of the great master. They opted for different strategies. Kahlo's work, unlike Rivera's, was small, personal and full of subtle emblems and ambiguous signs different from Rivera's directly symbolic political art, although both borrowed from traditional Mexican folk art – as Rivera himself put it Kahlo painted the inside, and he painted the outside. As usual Rivera nailed complex processes with a basic, blunt, down-to-earth phrase.

Modotti did the opposite – she submerged herself into Weston's formalist aesthetics to the point that their work was indistinguishable –then found her own voice by moving toward a more snapshot or documentary style. When asked by Carleton Beals, her good friend who was constantly writing in art journals – despite his prolific and complicated social/sexual life – just what she wanted to do with photography, she answered: "To make a perfect snapshot."[50] Can we then say that for Kahlo the subject was her private life and for Modotti it was the world outside on the street? No – and it is Laura Mulvey and Peter Wollen who explain why from their catalog *Frida Khalo and Tina Modotti*:

> Two points can be introduced here to break down this apparent polarity. First of all, the feminist slogan "the personal is the political" recasts Kahlo's private world in a new light. Secondly, Modotti's work as a photographer can only be understood in the context of her private life and position as a woman. The intention here then is to switch over, or rather to blur the distinctions set up by the polarity between them and to bring out the ways in which Kahlo's work is political, and Modotti's work is personal.[51]

As Mulvey and Wollen make clear in their concise and well thought out argument the two women have more in common than at first meets the eye.

Edward Weston, *Estridentista*?

The Aztec Land show led to an exhibit at another venue in Mexico City, on April 1924, at the avant-garde El Café de Nadie (Nobody's Café). This show was pivotal for Weston in many ways despite being a small group exhibit because of the friendship he developed with the artists Jean Charlot and Rafael Sala. The Spaniard Sala was an abstract painter and, like the Frenchman Charlot, who was a realist painter, spoke fluent English. The two men became Weston's closest friends during his stay in Mexico City. Along with Brenner and her circle, they were the principal people, aside from Modotti, that Weston saw regularly during his "Mexican period." Also in the show were masks by Germán Cueto and work by the young Fermín Revueltas who was a photographer, muralist and photomontage artist. Revueltas' work was influenced by *indigenismo*, Marxist politics, and contempt for traditional bourgeois aesthetics – as to be expected he usually showed mostly in radical journals and pamphlets rather than in galleries or museums.

The exhibit was curated by Maples Arce, the editor of *Irradiador* (*Irradiator*), a radical journal that published works aligned with the *Movimiento Estridentista* (*Movement of Stridents*). Arce was a Veracruzano and liked to scoot around town on a motorcycle in a beautiful suit, a dandy as well as an anarchist. As their name implied the art that they promoted was purposely aggressive, loud, harsh and grating. One of their slogans was "Chopin to the Electric Chair!" – a rallying cry sure to horrify parents, civic leaders, and concert pianists. They were fascinated by the new technology, including new forms of transportation, communication, and warfare, coming primarily from the US and Europe, which they saw in a positive light, as did the Futurists. For both groups the fusion of technology/war was seen as a purifying element, a "cleansing" that would bring forth a new kind of patriarchal society that would not simply dominate nature but ultimately supplant it.

The *Movimiento Estridentista* originated in Xalapa and sought to bring together elements of the then European avant-garde into Mexican art, especially their aspect of being provocateurs with exclusively modernist subject matter, such as electric trains, cars, airplanes and telephones. It then sought to fuse these subjects with an indigenous aspect that would be particular to Mexico. This last element overlapped with the *indigenismo* movement and this is where Anita Brenner and her circle, including Weston, came in.

To solidify Weston's alignment with the *Movimiento Estridentista*, *Irradiador* magazine used one of Weston's images for the cover of issue number 3. The picture – taking a page from Charles Sheeler's work – depicted smokestacks, in pinpoint focus, taken in October 1922 at the Armco Steel Company in Middletown, Ohio – Weston's first work to openly take advantage of the hard graphic edges that the Graflex camera could deliver, moving his work toward the kind of formalism that he would develop in Mexico. These were the pictures, along with the portraits, that had so impressed Stieglitz in 1922 when Weston came to New York with his portfolio. It is somewhat ironic that Weston was involved with *Irradiador* aesthetics since *indigenismo* was something he had no interest in. But his sharp focus pictures from Ohio did have an aspect of "hero-ism" that aligned itself (unintentionally) with both *Estridentista* aesthetics as well as Communist propaganda as we can see in Max Alpert's very similar photo of smokestacks that made the cover of *USSR In Construction* (1932), a propaganda journal published by the state. Similar photographs would crop up regularly in the USA and Europe throughout the 1930's. These pictures were all triumphalist, declaring unashamedly the ecstasy of industry, modernity, and progress.

This body of work by Weston's was enormously influential to Mexican photography, particularly to the work of Agustín Jiménez and Manuel Álvarez Bravo. One could even make a case that Jiménez, like Modotti, expanded on Weston's Mexican portfolio, taking that nascent formalism in a new and more daring direction more in tune with Russian and European photography but with a self-conscious Mexican flavor that was often playful and had an element of *indigenismo*. While Weston's cover for *Irradiador* perfectly fit the parameters of *Estridentista* aesthetics Weston did not share in the group's enthusiasm for modernity, for provocation, or for leftist politics. Mariana Figarella:

> "Weston was not interested in capturing images of Mexico's incipient modernity. Tina partially documented the changes that were transforming the traditional realities of Mexico City: The new stadium, the telegraphic cables that crisscrossed overhead, the scaffolding around the new buildings, the petrol tanks, objects that represented the new technology such as typewriters."[52]

As Figarella makes clear Modotti consistently photographed modernist, up-to-the-minute urban elements in Mexico City and Weston did not – even his highly regarded smokestack pictures from Ohio were of industrial factories that date to the mid-19th century. Nevertheless, Weston had gone in only a few years from Pictorialism, traditional portraiture, and dreary commercial work in Glendale, to participating in avant-garde exhibits and publications in Mexico. While he wasn't making much money he realized he was finally exactly where he needed to be, at the center of a photographic revolution from which there was no going back.

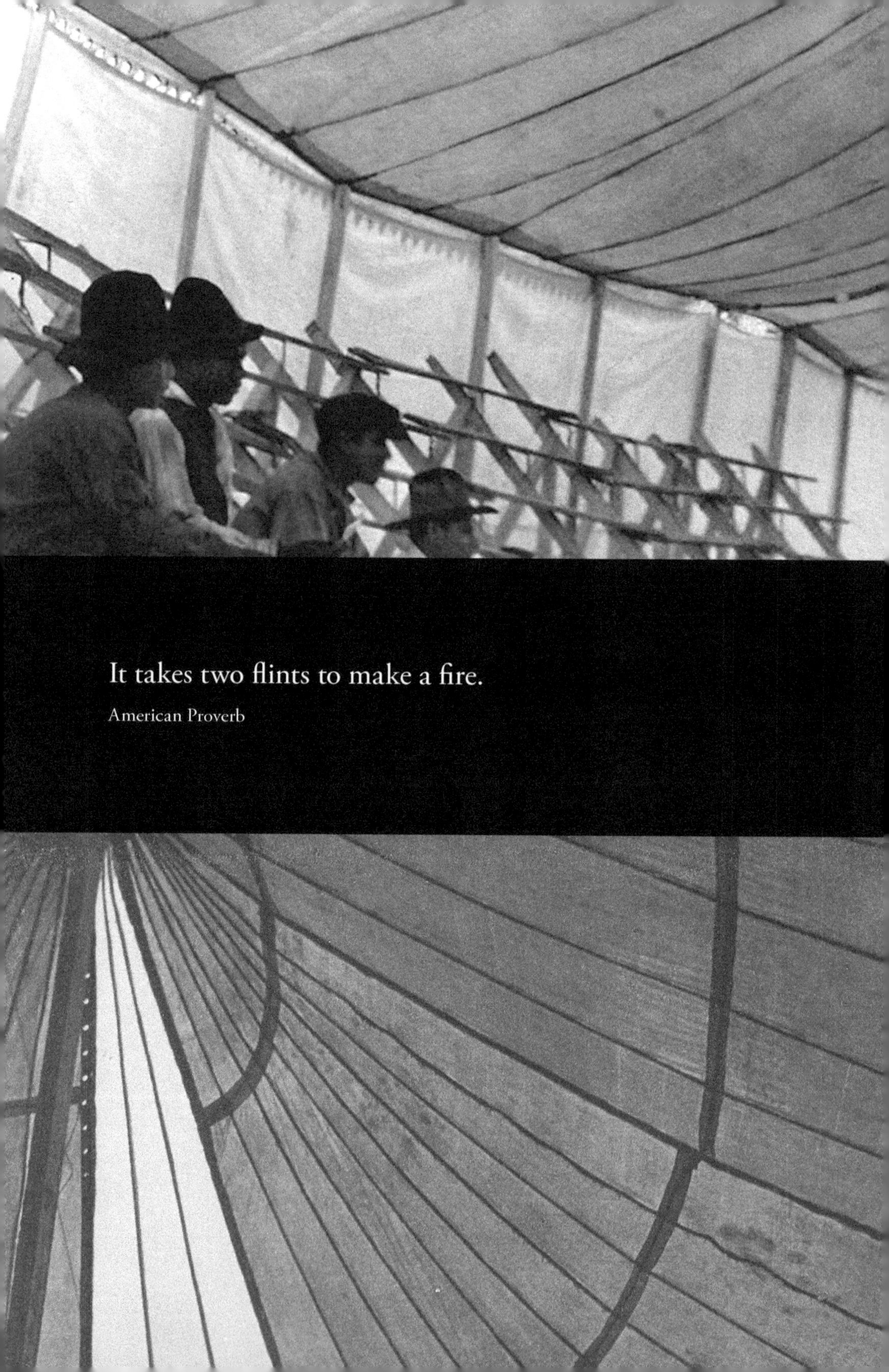

It takes two flints to make a fire.

American Proverb

05

Two Photographers Go to the Circus

The Circus Comes to Town

When a Russian circus came to town in the summer of 1924 and pitched its tent near their studio Weston and Modotti wandered over with his Graflex camera that both used to take pictures. Here we finally get to the point where Modotti and Weston are standing together with the same camera taking shots within a tightly controlled and lit space, and it is the similarities and the differences in their photographs that we need to address as it is key to understanding their work.

Weston's *Circus Tent* (1924) is one of the classic pictures in the canon of formalist photography. Rivera bought a print and hung it in his house. Looking up from ground level, the picture abstracts the big top tent into an arabesque of diagonal black lines that converge just off frame, top left. Large dark poles, asymmetrically framed at the far left and far right, contain the space like brackets.

In *Carpa de Circo, México* (*Circus Tent, México*) Modotti shoots from inside the same tent but there are four silhouetted spectators at the very bottom of the picture, half out of the frame, that anchor the image to the ground and give the picture an element of scale and psychology absent from Weston's picture. Modotti's camera placement makes the human subject the centerpiece of the work despite the oblique framing.

Edward and Tina Enter a Monastery

In their respective pictures of archways in a monastery Modotti's *Convento en Tepotzotlán* (1924) and Weston's *Convent Stairway and Skylight* (1924) the two photographers beautifully play off each other, like master jazz musicians trading lines in a duet. Modotti's *Convento en Tepotzotlán* was taken at an abandoned 17th- century Jesuit college and monastery at Tepotzotlán just north of Mexico City. Modotti's picture is seen as one of the high points of formalist photography in the Twenties and is the first picture that she showed publicly in a gallery. Modotti uses the archways and intersecting support structures as if they were repeating motifs in an abstract pattern of rounded edges butting up to hard diagonals. The pictures are of a convent, but also a formal arrangement in shades of gray. In one case the tones are daringly close together so that the photograph almost dissolves into a gray color-field abstraction.

With *Convent Stairway and Skylight* Weston pushes the dramatic aspect of intense light and heavy darkness meeting in the close quarters that are peculiar to churches and convents; his work is also more classically balanced, turning the stairs and skylight into space that is at first difficult to read. A hard shaft of strong light creates an upside-down pyramid shape that mirrors the skylight and plays off the black railing. His mastery of camera placement assures that he is able to turn this old stairwell into a complex series of intersecting points, lines and planes of black, white and gray – transferring the skylight into a work of abstract art. Weston and Modotti's formalism reaches its zenith here and we see that both of them seemed to savor the risk-taking of having their images dissolve into indeterminate, gray abstractions.

Roses and Tinfoil

Modotti's *Roses* (1924) pushes the formalist tropes toward a more personal iconography also seen in *Calla Lilies* (1925). While this grouping of objects that were the same or very much alike was commonplace in formalist photography – even becoming a school assignment at the Bauhaus in the 1930s under Lászlό Moholy-Nagy – in the right hands the motif might have the resonance and power of a painting by Paul Cézanne with uncertainty and directness sharing the stage. The French term "nature mort" might be more applicable than "still life" here as the convulsive confluence of sexuality and death seems to crowd the frame to overfull. One can feel that life/death struggle as the roses wither under the hard Mexican light. The photographer Agustín Jiménez learned much from Weston/Modotti, creating work that often follows in their footsteps (in his pictures of pyramids and marionettes), and from *Roses* he learned a great deal, as we can see in his work *Bolas de Loteria* (1933) that takes a more jaundiced view of fate.

Roses also leans toward abstraction in a way that others (including Jiménez) refused to do. This tendency reaches its zenith in Modotti's *Abstract: Crumpled Tinfoil* (1926) where the tinfoil creates an arabesque of shapes inside of shapes with a black hole at the bottom right, as if the universe itself were folding into darkness. The word "abstract" in the title acknowledges the formalism but the "tin foil" brings it back down to earth as tinfoil is a material found in kitchens that is inexpensive and commonplace as Modotti finds the transcendent and the sublime in the everyday. This was also Weston's hope for his own photography that he expressed in his *Daybooks,* that is, "to make the commonplace unusual."

Nautilus

To this end Weston took some seashells that Modotti had been collecting and turned them into still-life photographs that were minimal and monumental. The most famous of these pictures was not from Modotti's collection but belonged to the painter Henrietta Shore who painted seashells in her realist still-life work. Shore (originally from California) and Weston became close friends in the short three-year period that they were both in Mexico City. Weston's photograph is called *Nautilus* (1927) – after the name of the shell: Chambered Nautilus – and is one of the benchmark works of modernist photography. Shore's work was likewise inspired by Weston/Modotti as we can see in her painting *Women of Oaxaca* where a line of women wearing traditional clothing balance jugs on their heads.

Weston's idea with still-life is modernist to a fault as he believed that any subject or motif could be "completely outside subject matter" so, in effect, a seashell (or a rose) is not always a seashell (or a rose) thereby "taking one beyond the world we know in the conscious mind."[53] Is this heightened presence merely giddy formalist idealization or can an image take one to, or at least suggest, an underlying reality that is more "real" than mere surface reality? The question is an open one surely, but both Modotti and Weston sought answers with the medium of photography itself rather than rhetorically as in the more conceptual or illustrative art that we see in Dada and Surrealism.

Piñata

While Weston always played with his cards close to his chest when it came to his formalist aesthetic choices Modotti ventured out into the street with her Graflex portable camera. She did not do street photography in the classic sense of walking or driving and then shooting whatever seemed interesting but took a more carefully considered approach. She would find a good location for a shot, find the right angle for camera placement, then wait for passerby to come into her frame to shoot.

In one of her lesser-known masterpieces, *Piñata* (1926), she used this technique to photograph some large, almost life-size piñatas, made to resemble Charlie Chaplin, while some working-class men and boys wearing hats crowd the bottom of the frame. The busy image has wires, lights and Charlie's famous cane all vying for attention, as in a carnival fair but our eye goes immediately to the connection between Chaplin's simplified masklike face at the top and an *indigeno's* starkly realistic face in profile at the bottom. A rolled-up curtain at the very top of her frame turns the image into a work of theater – a curtain that is mirrored by a horizontal ledge at the bottom that separates the men from the piñatas. This picture goes far beyond anything being done in the US or Europe establishing Modotti as a master photographer – arguably her only equal now is Weston.

Pyramids and Dogs

While the Mexican pyramids had already been photographed extensively by 1924 no one had ever done it as well as Weston and none would equal him after. Incredibly he had no exposure to the pyramids until he went to photograph them. *Pirámide del Sol* (1924) accomplishes this feat through camera placement and brilliant darkroom work. Weston places the pyramid off-center right with some trees in the foreground. The bottom of his frame has some tall grass in bands of light and dark gray that act as a stage while the left side of the pyramid is in total darkness – this last part was accomplished by burning in the area in the darkroom but then also burning in the white clouds just to the side of this mysterious blackness, creating a motif there where the lightest most ephemeral part (clouds) meets the darkest most solid part (stone). It's a symphony of stone and clouds that Weston doesn't "capture," rather, he creates it. The photograph, as the critic Garcia suggested, evokes the fragmentation of Cubism but also looks further back to the proto-surrealist monumentality of Bruegel's *Tower of Babel* and also looks forward to Eisenstein's framing in *Que Viva Mexico!* – this last resemblance is not a coincidence as Eisenstein used Anita Brenner's *Idols Behind Altars* book as reference material in preproduction for his film so he was familiar with Weston/Modotti's work.

Modotti raises the stakes and even manages to make fun of Weston's formalism at the same time – one of her favorite photographic ploys in this period – in *Tree With Dog* (1924). Here Modotti focuses on a modernist courtyard seen from a few meters off the ground, so we are looking down at wet cement, in the shape of a pyramid, with a patch of grass that has a bare tree and a dog sitting by it, isolated, cautiously (tragically?) waiting. At the top part of the image is a very light white/gray that is also cement but might just be the sky behind the pyramid shape – the spatial play has the classical ambiguity of Braque and the sad absurdity of Beckett's *Waiting for Godot* and the "dog that came in the kitchen" song. One can sense here the delight in capturing the thing-itself and also a hunger for classical beauty in the composition and framing. The photograph also anticipates the dark humor in the surrealist work of Lee Miller from the 1930s, but the interplay of serious formalist tropes that lean to classical order and ambiguous, off-the-grid journalistic content that leans to mystery belongs purely to Modotti – she seems to be standing on the edge of something dangerous but is laughing at the same time, and that is very hard to do.

Rafael Sala by Modotti & Weston

She repeats these motifs of enigmatic overlit empty spaces in *Rafael in the Azotea* (1924), her insightful portrait of Rafael Sala, the Spanish painter who joined Weston's circle after arriving in Mexico in 1923. This shot seems to strangely anticipate the formalist, modernist framing of Michelangelo Antonioni's work from the 1960s where beautiful people find themselves in mysteriously empty "non-places," with italicized architectural motifs. Sala spoke fluent English as during World War I he had moved to New York and married the Spanish journalist and writer Monna Alfau. They honeymooned in Veracruz and from conversations with friends decided to travel to Mexico City to investigate the Mexican Renaissance. Like many others they stayed and became a part of it, Sala becoming involved in the muralist movement as chronicler and artist, also joining Rivera's circle of radical artists. Unfortunately, he contracted a fatal illness and died in 1927.

Modotti captures him formally posing on the *azotea* but the main subject at the bottom are two potted plants matched by two open windows in the background. Underneath the windows are some *indigenos* out of focus and partially blocked by the low wall. Modotti carefully sets up a psychological series of planes that isolate Sala between a "nature under control" (the potted plants) and another nature that is perhaps just starting to come into focus (the *indigenos*) between walls, screens and open windows that act as a series interconnected barriers and open spaces. In his black suit and hat Sala looks like he might be in mourning, waiting very still for Tina to tell him that he can go now – the sense of gravitas is palpable.

With these portraits Modotti moves beyond Weston's strict formalism as her work enters another aesthetic area altogether. In these pictures Modotti moves from making "easel art" to making highly personal "art-journalism" or, as she said herself, making "the perfect snapshot." More to the point Modotti by this time was treating the photograph as a *field* that could contain a variety of photographic codes or styles that included the snapshot. This was a choice necessitated by the obvious limitations of the various genres of photography and her desire to get the wholeness of the world, uncontained and contingent, into her work. For example, classicism tends to myth or mythologizing and documentary to "pure" factual evidence but Modotti wanted both at the same time. What she did was to treat the photographic negative as a *field* where one aspect could play off another, in a similar way that horns and strings may play off each other in a symphony, and in that clash of radical differences, create coherent, sometimes beautiful music. Modotti's discovery here is (as often happens) mirrored by similar photographic experiments around the same time in Europe and Russia.

Weston also took a series of pictures of Sala the same year and in the best of the series, *Rafael Sala* (1924), he is wearing the same black suit and hat, but carrying his artistic portfolio, the other hand in his pocket, pretending to walk forward in an interior space delineated only by a dark gray floor and a white wall – Weston daringly places Sala off-center far left as if he were just about to step out of the picture. The most interesting aspect of the photograph is the look on Sala's face as he looks behind him with some apprehension like an actor looking off-screen at something someone has just said. His immaculate coiffure and suit give him the look of a dandy out for a stroll but Weston places Sala literally against the white wall, his right shoulder just touching it, as if that wall were a translucent space that Sala was just about to cross, as in one of the Surrealist films then coming into their own, where walls and mirrors become portals into a metaphysical space.

Boy Wearing a Jorongo Cape

Weston and Modotti were at war with the clichés of portraiture as they sought to abolish anything that seemed either too pious or too picturesque; instead, they courted contradiction and complexity, and again their similarities and differences are telling. Arguably Modotti's most stunning anonymous portrait is *Boy Wearing a Jorongo Cape* (1928) that shows a young boy of about six wearing a straw hat at a rakish angle and a *jorongo* cape, or poncho, that falls down to his shoes that we can't see. Behind him are some enormous cactus plants that tower above him and reach beyond the picture plane. Modotti smartly opts to place the camera at the boy's eye level, placing him in the center of the frame, his face is impassive and seemingly already tired and much older than his years. Modotti does her own take on the monumentality of Rivera and Co. as the boy's frontality and placement within the frame turns him into a monolith. That she chose a small boy for this purpose shows Modotti working playfully within the tropes of classical representation but going her own way. It's one of the great portraits of the Twenties and seems to capture Mexican reality, its resilience and inscrutability, its sadness and stoicism, in a single shot.

Nahui Olin, Manuel Hernandez Galvan & Eliza

In 1923 Weston takes what many consider his greatest portrait, *Nahui Olin* (1923). Olin was the name Carmen Mondragón used throughout her life as an artist, writer, model and feminist provocateur – the name refers to the Aztec word for the movement of the cosmos. She was one of the first women to wear a miniskirt (before the term existed) in the 1920s and was a feminist and suffragette without regard for her conservative family – her father was a wealthy, politically conservative general. Her outspoken activism, sexuality and creativity were an affront to male bastions of power, and while Olin was a radical she eschewed Modotti's hardline politics, being more interested in psychology (principally her own), occultism, and art. Olin was an ambitious artist in her own right who showed her paintings alongside Frida Kahlo and Remedios Varo. Like many artists of the post-WWI Olin was also hyper-aware of her image in the media but resistant to the rules of the game; she wanted to be in the driver's seat when it came to how she was perceived but was naturally rebellious. While there were some master manipulators of public image then, such as the wily and ironic Salvador Dali and the cool and mysterious André Breton, most artists were just learning as they went along.

With *Nahui Olin* Weston opts for an aggressive, confrontational close-up using the almost square frame to full advantage as Olin's neck, head and flapper hairdo just barely touch all four sides of the frame, as if she were about to burst through the picture plane. He places the camera at the same level as her face and there is a wall directly behind her head so Olin seems trapped like a specimen sandwiched between the wall and the lens. What astonishes is the way Weston has captured her face, which is as expressive as any silent film actress but as realistic, direct and unposed as any snapshot. Her self-cut, feral, cropped hair and large green eyes, punctuated by her trademark loosely applied black eyeliner, makes her seem, at least in the many photographs that survive, more contemporary, and more fiercely alive, than anyone else from that time. Olin matches Weston's aggressive camera with a stare-down that would knock most photographers back a few feet. Nevertheless, Weston manages to hold his ground and gets the shot of his life in perhaps the greatest portrait of the decade.

Interestingly she disliked Weston's photograph (that everyone else loved), finding it too raw and intimidating – a characteristic then defined as "male" (in the conventions of photographic portraiture as well as in life). As a counter she produced her own photographic self-portrait where she looks like a typical Hollywood actress of the period, overly made up and theatrically lit with a cupid mouth carefully painted on – her face resembles an inscrutable Kabuki mask. Meanwhile Weston's picture is one where Mondragón/Olin's manifold personae – strong-willed, off-kilter, intelligent, eccentric, manic, obsessive and not suffering fools – were for one second all on her face and Weston got that one second forever in the amber of a black-and-white negative.

The following year the two repeat their photographic triumphs with Weston's *Manuel Hernández Galván Shooting* (1924) and Modotti's *Eliza Kneeling* (1924). Galván was a politician and a general in the revolutionary army – dangerous occupations that eventually got him assassinated. He had been in the midst of a reelection campaign and was ambushed while fraternizing in a Mexico City tavern – typical of Galván he went down shooting the revolver that he always carried with him just in case. His rugged masculinity attracted many women, including Modotti, who had a brief liaison with him. Weston shows Galván aiming one of his guns during a target practice session – he appears completely self-possessed, self-assured and unselfconscious. Weston presses the shutter at just the moment Galván fires, creating one of the great iconic images of Mexican masculinity.

In Modotti's *Elisa Kneeling* the subject was Elisa Ortíz, the Guadalajaran maid that Weston and Modotti had hired from the beginning of their stay in the city. She fell in love with Weston during their three years together but it is not known if he took advantage of that fact. Elisa was also a strict Catholic and so tortured by her love for a man who had a family in California with a wife and children as well as a mistress in Mexico City who was her boss. The romance caused havoc for her and she was devastated when he left. In *Elisa Kneeling* Modotti photographed her wearing all black, as if mourning, and looking not much older than a adolescent but already prematurely sad and holding one hand with the other as if comforting herself – Modotti was always conscious of hands and their secret language. Her strangely awkward, almost painful, pose is beautifully human, somewhat masochistic, strangely energized and stoic in equal measure. *Elisa Kneeling* is one of Modotti's great portraits in its subtle insistence on seeing women as complex, contradictory beings in the world rather than merely models.

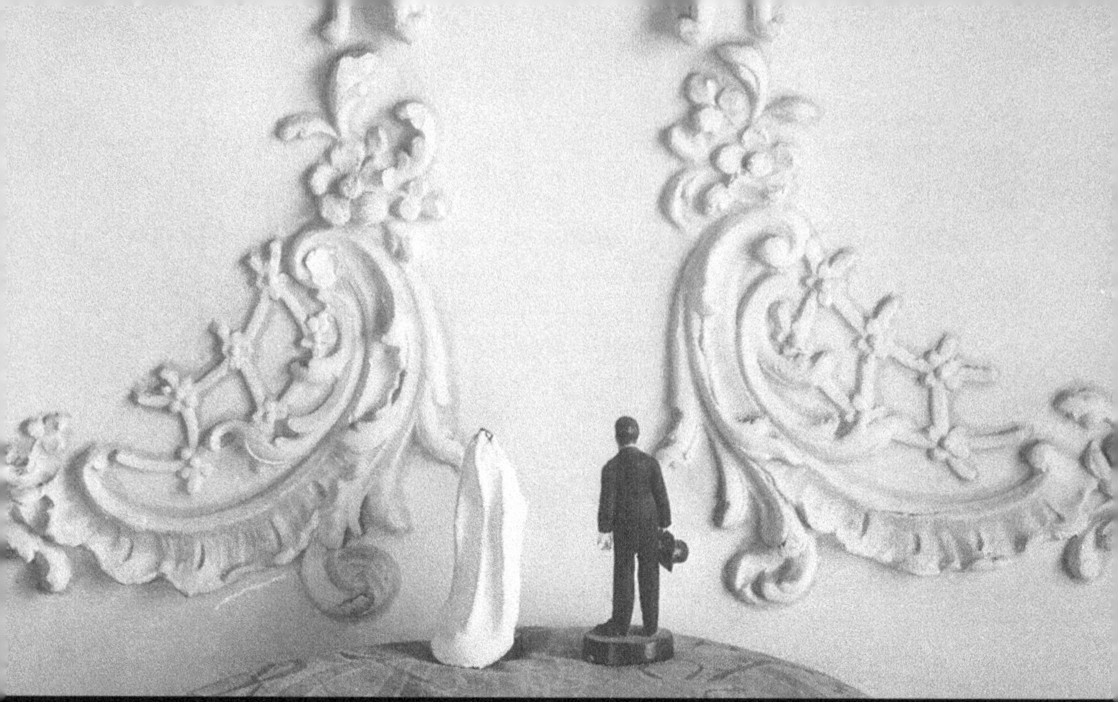

Marriage is a wonderful institution,
but who wants to live in an institution?

Groucho Marx, *Groucho and Me, the Autobiography*

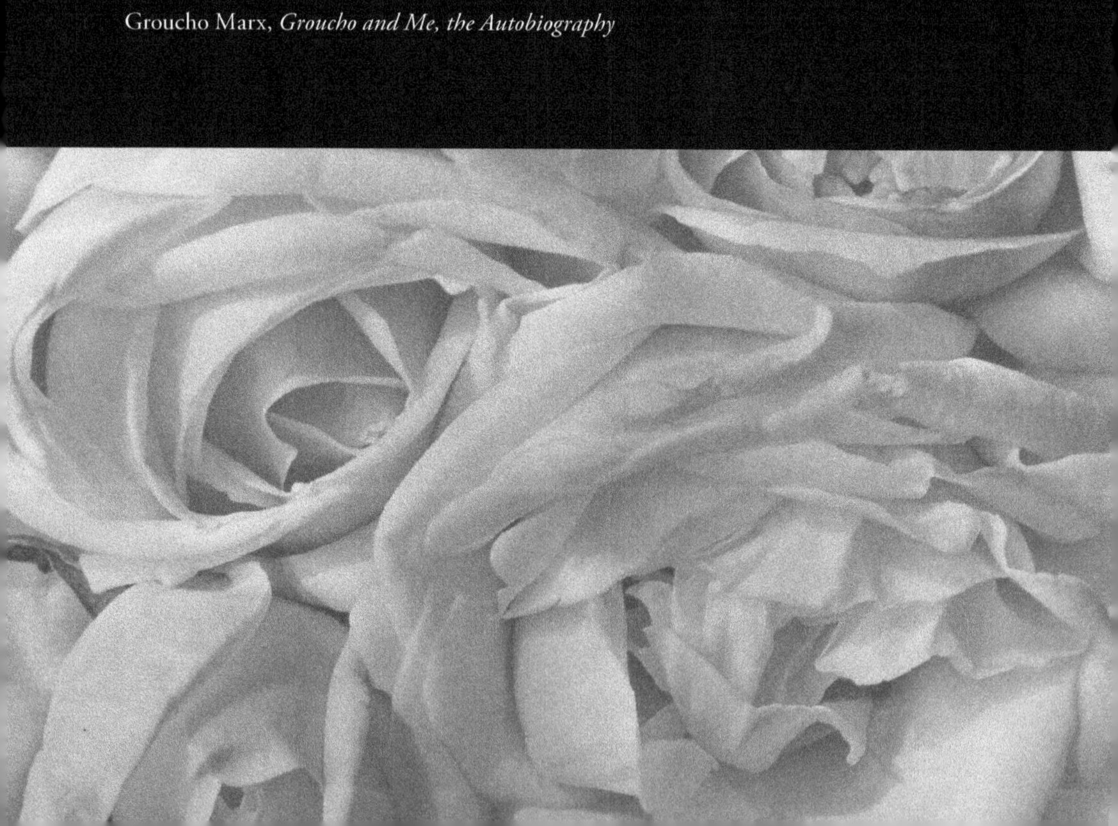

06

A Marriage Portrait Without a Marriage

Tina Reciting

Before and after his "Mexican period" Weston had an insistent, one might say set-to-default, manner of treating women, particularly his models, as occasional objects of desire. That changed with Modotti. He saw her as an autonomous subject, an equal and a partner, and this change produced arguably his best work as we see in his magnificent series *Tina Reciting* (1924). This is a cycle of pictures that show Modotti reciting her favorite poems from memory in tight, unforgiving close-ups that give a full account of her expressive face. This body of work is meant to suggest a sequence of film stills conveying a series of subtle, contradictory, often mysterious emotions that all seem, unlike traditional portraiture, undecided and in the middle of an action. Weston doesn't just make a new body of work here but opens the door to a new genre of photography where the chaos and vulnerability, the defiance and wonder, the *recklessness* of the moment, are not just allowed into the picture, but rather, they make the picture.

Later rock-and-roll photography is unthinkable without Weston first showing people where the door was. When Bob Moreland photographed Elvis Presley pausing to get his breath, eyes closed in ecstasy, in 1955 during his revolutionary *Sun Sessions,* or when Jim Marshall photographed Ray Charles laughing his ass off during a recording session in New York City in 1960, Weston gets a credit. Moreland and Marshall both understood, as a matter of course, the importance of getting *in-between* the decisive moments, the casual gestures, the throwaway instants that are gone in a flash.

In the series *Tina Reciting* Modotti's acting skills come to the fore as does Weston's moody lighting that punctuates her dramatically beautiful face with deep shadows and a dark background that emphasizes the theatrics, but the main accent of the pictures is on her movement with facial expressions in medias res. In the Hollywood of the Twenties they sometimes made silent versions of plays, including Shakespeare, relying on the actor's ability to express the ideas and emotions, and so it is here.

Weston here goes flat-out against the norm (then and now) where portraiture is suggestive of a coherent psychology, of a spiritual facticity, of an "essence." Even people with no direct knowledge of photography have learned these obligatory conventions and apply them when posing, knowing that the photographer expects them. Those conventions were solidly in place when Edward Steichen photographed Greta Garbo in 1928 (*Greta Garbo in Hollywood*) and they were in place when Beth Garrabrant photographed Taylor Swift in 2020 (*Taylor Swift Midnights Press Shot 2*). Weston and Modotti here energetically reject these conventions and take an existential approach (before the term existed), that is, they suggest that existence precedes essence so there is no predetermined purpose, nature or meaning. It should not surprise us that Weston/Modotti anticipated existentialism, as philosophy is always (hopelessly) playing catch-up.

Modotti here creates her essence and meaning through action, through speech, through an expression of her own radical freedom. Never have a photographer and a model worked more closely together to create a work of art that aspires not to perfection or to glamour but to the unfiltered reality of a moment between two people, or even the moment between the moments.

Heroic Heads

In this period Modotti and Weston can do no wrong as they produce masterpieces in several genres of photography on an ongoing basis. Weston also completes a whole body of work titled *Cabezas Heroicas* (*Heroic Heads*) inspired by his portrait of Olin. As the title makes clear the *Cabezas Heroicas* are conceived as monumental images – the head fills the frame on all sides. No concessions are made to the sitter's desires to appear beautiful, intelligent or charming. Facial features are seen frontally with no props, or stylish outfits. His first *Heroic Head* subject was Rivera's first wife, Lupe Marín – a woman who fascinated Weston, as she did many others. Elena Poniatowska devoted a great novel, *Dos Veces Única* (*Two Times Unique*) to her life story. *Heroic Heads* remains the most radical and extraordinary series of portraits of the early century – mostly of the exiles, artists and bohemians living in the Mexico City of the Twenties.

Modotti and Weston: the *Azotea* Pictures

Despite Weston's radical visual vocabulary with regard to portraiture undoubtedly his best-known body of work from this period are the nudes/portraits that he made of Modotti in 1924. The pictures that they did together in the *azotea,* the roof of their house in Mexico City, are masterpieces of the genre(s) that are still radical today due to the fact that Weston has imploded the dividing line between portrait and nude – something no one had done before because the conventions of the two seemed incompatible – to a very great extent it is still that way today. This separation was something that was not enforced, in the traditional sense, but was seen as simply "normal" and so everyone followed along. Weston not only ignores that dividing line but does it with seeming effortlessness and then proceeds to make something new from this transgression.

With Modotti as co-creator he confronts her directly with his camera and makes the expressions on her face often as important as her nude body as Tina usually looks into the lens knowingly. She also chose her own way to pose her body and the location, in a sense art directing the shot. What then followed was a dance of sorts between photographer and model where they try to find the image that will work best at that moment – one gets a sense of the liberating freedom of this approach, something that jumps off the page.

This is Mariana Figarella writing about one of those nude/portrait works:

> In one image, until recently little known, *Tina Con El Torso Desnudo* (1924) (*Tina With Nude Torso*) we are half way between portrait and nude...This photograph is doubly daring: for its composition as well as its unusual eroticism...We appreciate a wise conjunction of a modern aesthetic in its search for a synthesis, for a structure, and its aftertaste of Symbolism with its decadent discharge, exoticism, and their taste for depicting beautiful women as fatal seductresses...Tina appears semi-clothed in a kimono, with her hair disheveled and with an ambiguous expression (seen in Symbolist art) oscillating between a mystical ecstasy and the erotic, signified by the hands at the same level as her breasts.[54]

Figarella's spot-on take of Weston's photograph is impressive but she leaves out the cinematic aspect as the picture also looks like a film still from a postcoital scene between two lovers. This narrative subtext is important to the work's overall success as it creates a beautiful tension with the Symbolist tropes that Figarella describes so well.

Once again, we see Weston working with ambiguity and suggestive mise en scène. Aside from being both portrait and nude, the pictures are tightly composed and improvisational, erotically charged and reflective, capturing the moment-itself but also seemingly in transition from one movement to another – *in between* an action. This in between suggests a state of constant flux, ambiguity, perhaps disorientation – the "between" might also be that mediating space between finitude and transcendence. Weston didn't just illustrate those ideas but expressed them on a two-dimensional plane of black and white. More to the point he did not accomplish this extraordinary sleight of hand by himself. Modotti understood Weston's art and assisted in the construction of this existential, modernist body of work. It was as if her complaints about Hollywood had been answered and she was finally acting and collaborating with an artist in work that was worthy of both of them.

It should not come as a surprise that feminist criticism has taken Weston to task for the *azotea* pictures without taking into account Modotti's collaboration, strangely seeing her as a passive odalisque. In her book *Tina Modotti: Image, Texture, Photography* Andrea Noble quotes the film historian and theoretician Laura Mulvey: "Woman could be the bearer of meaning, not the maker of meaning."[55] Just how one can achieve one without the other is something neither Noble nor Mulvey explain, since it seems likely that everyone, male or female, who is alive and conscious is both making meaning and bearing meaning at all times, even if they are not aware of it – those who are aware (at times to the point of self-consciousness) are sometimes referred to as artists.

Modotti's and Weston's work in the *azotea* series would have no equals either in their own time or in a subsequent comparable body of photography – a remarkable achievement since, by now, the number of female nudes must number in the billions. The only work that comes even close is to be found in films, most obviously in Ingrid Bergman and Roberto Rossellini's collaborations in their magnificent series of works (*Stromboli/Europe '51/Journey to Italy*). In these films Bergman barely takes off her coat much less her clothes but it is her face that is brutally naked. This trilogy from 1950 to 1954 would be beautifully reconstructed and deconstructed by Jean-Luc Godard with Anna Karina in the 1960s starting a new chapter for the medium. That cinema should take up the torch lit by Weston/Modotti makes a lot of sense as avant-garde filmmakers felt an affinity for avant-garde photography while conventional photographers themselves were not up to the task, falling into the same traps repeatedly to the point of banality and oblivion.

Weston in his *Daybooks* from the 1940s, when he was in California, remembered the *azotea* pictures from 20 years previously in some detail when he hears of Tina's death in January 1942. Weston again seems to have discarded the diary entries but they were recovered by his neighbor Dewitt Hughes while he was searching for pictures in the trash; these were later transcribed by the Southern California Architectural History blog. The entries have the typical matter-of-fact realities next to romantic poetic asides typical of Weston:

> Tina is sunbathing on the *azotea* of the hacienda. I have been writing correspondence to the art world in the US to remind them that I am still alive and photographing. I take leave of my study for a breath of fresh air and steal upon Tina sunbathing on the worn stone tiles. I quickly head back for the Graflex, quietly set up the tripod, align the camera to the most advantageous position, all without interrupting the silence of Tina's repose.
>
> There she is, hand covering her eyes from the sun, her dark brown nipples standing erect, nearly matching the hue of the blanket beneath her. I peer through the glass. My hand reaches for the cable release. Tina is angelic, an angel drifting in the realm of angels.
>
> "Are you finished now?" Tina says.
> "You pretender, I thought you were asleep," I say.
> "I was until you came along with all your racket. Did you really think I could sleep?"
> "Come now, it wasn't as bad as all that."
> She sits up, still covering her eyes. Her breasts fall like fruit onto her belly.
> "Do you want to take any more? How should I sit?""
> "What's the point now?" I say, trying to outdo her. "You've ruined the mood. I'll even have to destroy the negative."
> "You must be mad, why?"
> "It would be dishonest to."
> "Nobody will know the difference," she says as she leans back onto her elbows, supine and seductive.
> "No, I suppose they never will."[56]

Tina's more practical, feminist jabs against Weston's exasperated male romanticism seem exactly as they were described by friends of the period. Weston's text provides comical but also useful context for their workaday routine and their relationship, making it clear that their lives and their art were one, that is, they were *living with* the camera rather than simply using the camera.

Escusado and *Lineas Telefonicas*

Interestingly, for the titles in this period Weston used the Spanish words rather than the English, suggesting that he was now immersed in Mexican culture, even if he never learned the language. In 1925 Weston produced *Escusado* (*Toilet*). In his *Daybooks* from this period he seems to have been taken with the then new term "form follows function" and sought ways to apply it to photography. His frequent visits to see Rivera working with Modotti shooing the work, and his long talks with Brenner and Charlot would suggest as much. Over a span of two weeks he photographed the toilet from different angles eventually removing the wooden toilet seat for the final image. Weston was knowledgeable about art history and understood exactly what he was doing – in his *Daybooks* he likened the toilet itself to the *Winged Victory of Samothrace,* the famous sculpture that is one of the shining stars in the Louvre's collection.

The friends who saw the work commented favorably upon it, including Modotti, who considered it Weston's best work up to that point. Jean Charlot told him it was one of the most "sensitively observed" works he had ever seen. Another friend, Pablo O'Higgins, concurred and added that the work signaled a new chapter for Weston.[57] Pablo was born Paul Stevenson in Salt Lake City, a Mormon center and one of the most conservative cities in the US. Like so many others, including Charlot, he had come to Mexico to remake himself and take part in the Mexican Renaissance. O'Higgins established the Taller de Gráfica Popular (The People's Graphic Workshop) – a graphic studio that specialized in leftist political illustrations and posters influenced by the muralists and *indigenismo*.

Diego Rivera had perhaps the most savvy art historical comment about *Escusado*: "In all my life I have not seen such a beautiful photograph. It is in some ways like Marcel Duchamp's urinal (*Fountain*, 1917) but better."[58] Rivera was right. Duchamp's *Fountain* would signal the opening chapters of conceptual art, installation art, and institutional critique art – one might even say it provided a template for these dominant fine art forms in the later part of the century and beyond –but Weston's is arguably the better artwork. While Duchamp's *Fountain* has the single-mindedness of a one-note joke (a feature beloved by fine-art aficionados), Weston's picture comes down to earth (literally) to carefully examine the contours, the strangeness, and the beauty of a specific Mexican toilet. The picture has the gravitas of a still life by Chardin, the clarity of a photograph of the new industries by Charles Sheeler and the ironic humor of Picasso.

Something that is obvious but that Rivera failed to mention, perhaps out of modesty, is that Weston had clearly learned some lessons from the Mexican master muralist. *Escusado* is flagrantly monumental but it forces this monumentality into a small scale suffusing it with irony and formal detachment, unlike Rivera's work which was direct, confrontational and political. Other artists were also using these ideas around the same time, such as Georgia O'Keeffe in her iconic monumental flower paintings, but O'Keeffe's work is patently heroic seeing nature (or Nature) as feminine, primal, and *fundamental* while Weston's *Escusado* is an homage to a humble, simple, utilitarian object. It has the clarity and directness of an American pragmatist looking intently at the everyday world, similar in some respects to the poetry of William Carlos Williams, who wrote poems in praise of ordinary objects, such as a wheelbarrow.

Something else we must consider is that Weston had de-politicized Rivera's monumentality and pushed it to become a part of his formal vocabulary – simply another arrow in his quiver. The lessons of *Escusado* would last Weston for the rest of his life and serve him well. Let's take an example from 1930, *Pepper,* made four years after his return to California. *Pepper* is part of a whole series of works with this title produced that year and is one of the most popular pictures in American culture, still selling as original prints (produced later by the Weston family) and as posters and postcards. With *Pepper* the small scale and intimacy of the sensuous pepper is in contrast to its seemingly monumental scale that Weston achieved through camera placement, lighting and focus.

Such pictures would be unthinkable without the work of Rivera and the muralists. But this monumentality was not necessarily welcome in the North as a matter of course, as Rivera discovered. The artist traveled to New York City in 1932 with his wife, Frida, who like her Marxist circle of friends liked to refer to the US as *Gringolandia*. Rivera had been invited to paint a mural at the entrance to Manhattan's Rockefeller Center to be titled *Man at the Crossroads* – construction on the iconic building had begun a year earlier in

1931 and would take several years to complete. The subsequent outrage, due to the obvious Marxist references, featuring an idealized portrait of Lenin, along with satires of capitalist culture, was so shocking to the Rockefeller family that they ended up destroying the mural. While the Rockefellers could easily afford to pay Rivera off and tell him, in so many words, to go home, other commissions quickly retired their offers fearing backlash, forcing Rivera and Kahlo to return to Mexico. But Rivera had the last laugh as he remade the mural in Mexico but added a caricature of Rockefeller as one of the evil forces of capitalism found at the omnipresent "crossroads."

Weston's *Pepper* received a more heartfelt welcome when an original print made by Weston was purchased as part of the permanent collection at the Metropolitan Museum in Manhattan, about 20 blocks from Rockefeller Center. Clearly in the US there was an appropriate and acceptable monumentality and one that was not to be tolerated. Rivera and Weston would stand at the opposite ends of a political struggle that would test the friendship between the two artists. Perhaps it was fortunate that neither man spoke the other's language, so they were able to remain friends despite Rivera's heartfelt commitment to Communism.

Upon seeing *Escusado* Modotti studied it carefully and that same year matched Weston with her own masterpiece *Lineas Telefonicas*. Her competitive fire was rarely discussed in the biographies as Tina was always described as soft-spoken, with a "sweet" voice and a self-deprecating sense of humor. But in terms of her art she was absolutely fearless, scrappy and committed – she held her ground and looked to be the best without qualifications about "being a woman." As Figarella pointed out Modotti's choice is telling. While the toilet is pre-modern, dating from 1596, telephone wires could not exist before the 20th century.

Lineas Telefonicas dives into modernism head on as Modotti knew this was Weston's weakness – she knew that he would stay away from these motifs because he felt uneasy around them, they put him off. *Lineas Telefonicas* is also, like *Escusado,* monumental, turning a simple telephone pole with wires into a totemic sculpture – as if she were photographing one of the massive stone deities of Aztec culture she had seen while traveling through Mexico. She achieves this through high contrast printing, camera placement, and framing the pole/wires in the center of her frame as she looks up from ground level. This extraordinary work has the "adoration of the modern" typical of the *Estridentistas* and the Futurists but also an underlying sense of tragedy as if she were an anthropologist photographing the ruins of a civilization long gone, wondering what those strange wires were for.

Nudes and Portraits of Anita Brenner

With *Anita Brenner (Nude Back)* 1925 Weston created what he thought was the best work he had ever made. The series of pictures depict Brenner's nude back and buttocks, with her head unseen tilted down. The shape of the torso is reminiscent of a pear and Weston contrasts that hard graphic shape to a black background. This expressive, single-minded work would become the template for his photography dealing with female nudes for the remainder of his life and in that sense one can see why he thought it was the most important work of his life up to that point. Modotti also photographed Anita Brenner the same year but they are portraits – arguably the best of Brenner's unusual, beautiful face. They take a page from Weston's *Heroic Heads* series but have their own sense of movement within the frame lacking from Weston's work as Brenner stretches her long neck turning it into part of the drama of the photograph. Her face, sans makeup and confrontational with the camera, makes no concessions to conventions of beauty or "posing" as such. They are the rawest and most direct, in-your-face portraits Modotti ever did – again treating a woman as an independent autonomous subject with her own identity and vision. Brenner looks like a formidable, fearless iconoclast ready for all comers and Modotti gets the beauty of that intense energy into her picture.

Absorbing the Other

With *Escusado* and *Lineas Telefonicas* along with their portraits of this period it becomes clear that Modotti and Weston are pushing each other toward the avant-garde, but not out of any ideological commitment, since that was something that Weston at least was fundamentally adverse to. There was a tension that was in perfect balance between Modotti's humanism and Weston's formalism as they were both pushing to control the aesthetic direction of their pictures but also seeking to accommodate, control and absorb the other.

That is, Weston had learned his lessons from Mather and Stieglitz and was pushing himself and Modotti toward a formalist aesthetic, but one that was open to ambiguity and paradox. The work shifted gears from irony to emotional directness, from hot confrontation to cool detachment, and from obsessive framing to a snapshot aesthetic with ease, as if he were shifting gears on a car. This is why many at the time considered Weston the best photographer in the US. Weston in this period was using every trick in the book, as he wanted to get the complexity and contingency of the world into his pictures. He would only cover himself in the golden robes of "formalist master" in his later years but the initial impetus for that formalist work was established in Mexico with his photographs of Anita Brenner.

In turn, Modotti took that formalism and applied it to humanist urban motifs, everyday life and modern people who were navigating through the new century – she was determined to find her own way. As Antonio Machado, Modotti's favorite poet, put it in a famous quote that she liked to repeat: "There is no path – paths are made by walking." Modotti made her own path. This pushed Weston to confront contemporary humanist subject matter that would have normally been outside of his purview. The fact that he never returned to this more of-the-moment, socially conscious subject matter that included aspects of the "snapshot aesthetic" in his later work makes it clear that it was an aspect of his "Mexican period" under the influence of Modotti.

As each artist sought to absorb the strengths of the other they met in the middle, and it is in this vague "middle" that sparks flew. By a strange paradox each artist produced not only their best pictures during those three years but also their most personal work. They needed each other desperately but seem to have been oblivious to this fact – each treating the other as a friend, a casual lover, and an occasional collaborator, but they were unaware that, like Braque and Picasso, they were roped together climbing a steep, dangerous mountain – one might say that being unaware they fell.

Edward and Tina: a Wedding Portrait

As for their relationship Modotti well realized that Weston's marriage to Chandler was not particularly important to him, but his kids were – he missed them and wanted to be a family man, making a return to California at some point inevitable. Neither spoke about it but each was waiting for the other shoe to drop. As a result they maintained a close relationship but were wary of being hurt when the time came to say goodbye and so were also keeping each other (emotionally speaking) at arm's length.

Neither Modotti nor Weston ever took a picture of themselves together as a couple, perhaps considering such portraits sentimental and bourgeois. She took rather formal portraits of him, looking quite serious with his pipe and camera, and he of course took many pictures of her – but there were no pictures of them together. Fortunately for us they were, at least, aware of this lack. Margaret Hooks: "On the anniversary of their first year in Mexico, at Tina's suggestion she and Edward went to a professional photographer to have a joke 'wedding portrait' made. Tina holds a dusty bunch of fake flowers against her cheek as the happy couple poses against a romantic backdrop both trying desperately to control their mirth."[59] A professional photographer advertising his wares, with various "backgrounds" available for portraiture, was found but it was Modotti, as usual, who took the initiative – the fact that they treated their wedding picture like a joke is telling. When they entered the photography studio she said, tongue firmly in cheek: "We have just been married today – el señor is very religious, perhaps you can make it with a church in the background."[60]

At least three of the pictures survive. In one they are indeed posed with a painted backdrop of an ersatz medieval cathedral; in the other it is the more traditional park setting. In the first Weston is sitting wearing a suit and Modotti, in a simple blouse and skirt, is holding a bouquet of fake flowers with one hand and touching Weston's shoulder with the other as was the tradition then in photo portraiture of couples. In another picture Modotti is looking off into space, head at an angle, while Weston, in awe, turns to look in her direction almost afraid to confront her gaze. They are both charming pictures that capture their sense of adventure, of sharing the same sense of the absurd, of thumbing their noses at bourgeois convention, but the pictures also do what they are supposed to do, that is, they commemorate a love story through the medium of photography. It is a great irony that an unknown photographer selling his wares near the central marketplace in Mexico City photographed two of the greatest photographers of the century. His pictures would become the only studio photographs we have of "Edward and Tina."

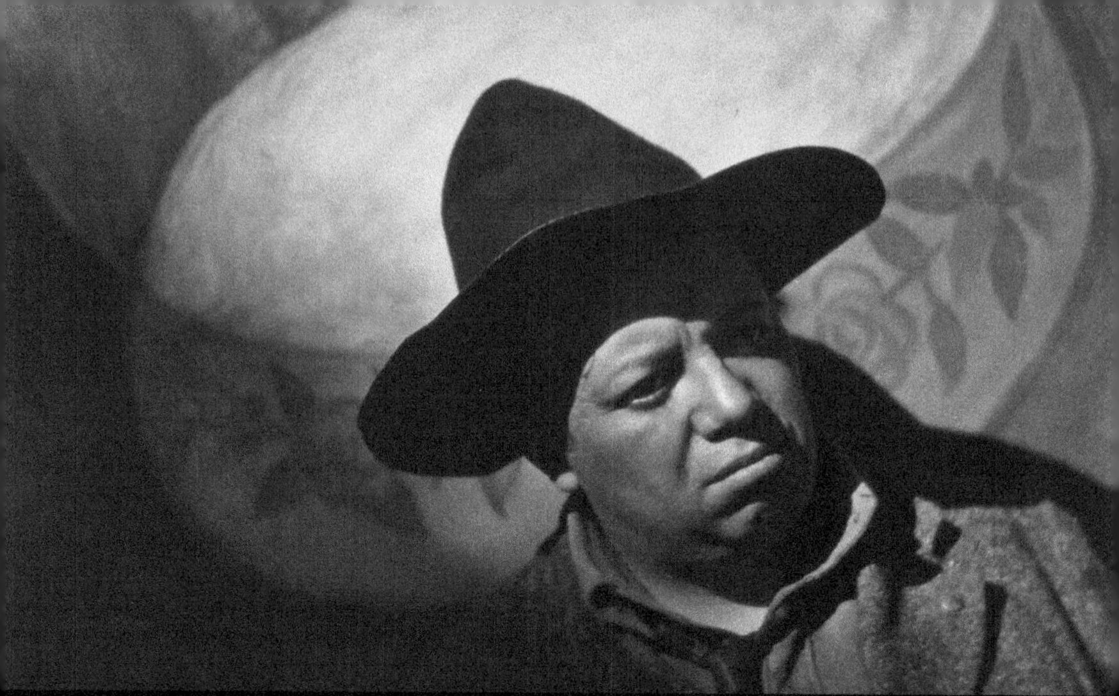

They'll eat your heart alive. Every time.

Jack Kerouac, *Mexico City Blues*

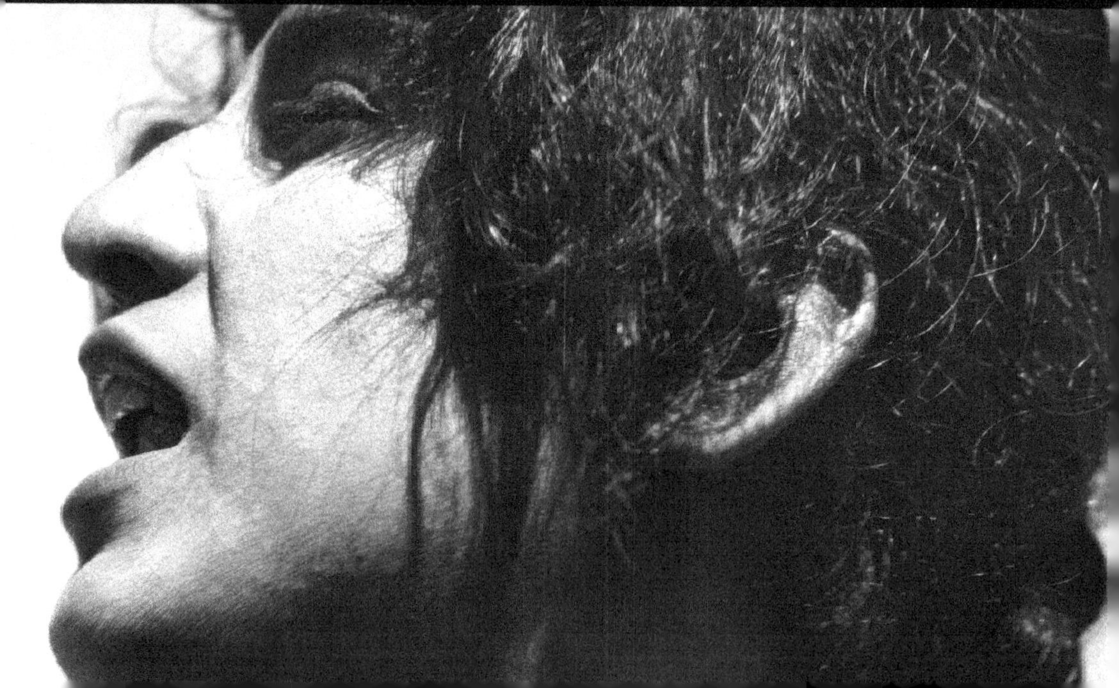

07

Mexico City Nights

A Night With Lupe Marín & Diego Rivera

Lupe Marín, Rivera's wife for a period, was known for many things: her beautiful green eyes, her direct no-nonsense manner of speaking, her ability to hold her liquor and talk endlessly into the night, her beautiful legs, her sense of humor and intelligence, her large hands, her crushing put-downs – one could go on. She was the Ava Gardner of Mexico before that star started to shine later in the century. Her late-night get-togethers have passed from Mexican history into Mexican folklore. In her book *Tinísima* Elena Poniatowska re-creates one of those long evenings in prose using all of her narrative skills to give an idea of what they were like – Lupe's chapter is extensive and features many names from that time which have gone into oblivion, but Poniatowska does a great job of using sudden turns and twists in the language, full of fragmented speech and oblique, suggestive descriptions, including euphemisms and colloquialisms peculiar to the time/place, to give a good sense of the party and its guests. I would like to give you here an abridged version translated by me so one gets at least a glimpse of Modotti and Weston's charmed life which is important in understanding what it is they had, and what they lost. The evening begins in the kitchen of Marin's/Rivera's home – from *Tinísima*:

> "I don't think you brought enough cheese," suggested Tina. "Half a kilo is not enough? You're Italian so you're a cheeseaholic...maybe you're right. They're all big eaters." With her apples in the air and her buns tight Lupe crossed her shawl over herself. "Won't be long, while I'm gone move those little hands over to the chopping block...Ahh cilantro! Gotta get cilantro." From the *azotea* Weston saw Lupe moving away from the house like a panther, leaving behind her undulating waves that were strangely disturbing. The quiet air that Lupe left behind her was gray. He could see in the kitchen Tina and Elisa cleaning radishes. Lupe returned loaded with packages. "What, no one's here? Couple of asses – do I have to do everything?"

Dalila and Maria Orozco Romero announced themselves at six and María whispered to Tina: "God I can't take my sister's screeches!" Lupe screamed out, "pair of idiots, what's the matter with you? Look at the time. Here the Italian has sweated like a pig. Mules! You're finally here and the guests are arriving.

The long, tall figure of Fito Best Maugard, accompanied by two beauties, Maria Asúnsolo and her cousin Lolita caused a shuddering tempest that ricocheted around the room. The moment Weston saw them he ran for his dictionary so he could speak to the "*bellas señoritas*." A senator with mariachis carrying pistols greeted everyone simultaneously with a raised hand exclaiming "Pancho Villa, the most beloved man in Mexico, salud!" "And Ricardo Gómez Robelo?" asked Tina. Gómez Robelo, as everyone knew, was consumed with a fire for Tina. Even the minister of Education José Vasconcelos said that his fever was all Tina's fault.

Anita Brenner and Frances Toor brought Nahui Olín, well tequilaized, her immense green eyes more violent, more aggressive than *ever* because Dr. Atl had left her stranded without notice – "That fucking midget will pay for that mistake." Olín fell in love with Rodriguez Lozano. But he's not aware at all. Just like her there are a lot of fluffed chickens, cluck, cluck, cluck, cluck, stupid and blind, pathologically fertile." When Nahui saw the most handsome cadet in the whole of the Military Academy she asked her father to give him as a gift. "Really Nahui?" With her bun and her Chinese paper.

Elisa Guerrero gave the gift of her eyes to Weston but he had eyes only for Diego Rivera. The pistol at his side contrasted with his warm, wan smile. Diego explained: "All Mexican artists are Communists, well, the good ones. They call me the Lenin of Mexico. We're not café Communists but the real thing." Weston called to Chandler who was glued to Elisa's skirt like a lapdog. "Look at that man, he's a genius. Look at his head, he has a wide forehead, an immense dome, look closely, the head of a thinker." Diego didn't shut up and then would suddenly let out an enormous laugh.

When Lupe arrived she let out a rapid-fire whistle. "Big guy, you have tits like an old woman – and I guess since I have none we make a good pair." She looked at her own breasts: "Titties like a snake." The theme of "tits" was recurrent in Lupe's talks. After the meal Diego announced that Lupe and Hernández Galván would sing songs.

> At dawn, in peace, in front of his diary, Weston would try to take account of everything and see if it added up. Mexico, a country prone to fires, even the water was sometimes on fire. Tina at the center of it all. If Tina had seen his diary it would have caused open stupefaction to discover his deep jealousy. To Tina Edward was the same man he was in Los Angeles. In Mexico she was indispensable. She was the giver, the distributor of plenty. He didn't speak Spanish; they spent most of the day together, he depended on her. My "*Aztequita*." His nights were better than in LA. She ignored Weston's poetry, full of spite.
>
> Julio Torre only had eyes for Tina, he would follow her around unable to hide his feelings. "Him too? said Weston. Diego had a new diet: only strawberries. When Lupe returned she curtly ordered immediately: "Culture night is *over*, now we relax and sing some songs! I planted a leek and up came a creeeeep! What's the matter with you all? Is this a party or what? Well, let's party." When it got very dark Lupe was still singing. The waiters were holding on to the curtains, their hands very still, their napkins held tightly in their fists, they didn't move."[61]

So much for the nights – let's return to the days and leave Poniatowska's beautiful prose behind to look more closely at the respective collaborative work of Weston and Modotti as they became well-known in Mexico through newspapers and magazines seen on a regular basis, for that is how most people then would have seen their work, not in gallery or museum shows.

Magazine Work

For both Modotti and Weston portraits and magazine work were not only viable as exposure but also necessary forms for generating income as Chandler's monthly allowance barely covered costs. In the Twenties magazines were seen as a way not only to make money but to acquire wealth. While now that idea would be preposterous in that time famous writers (Scott Fitzgerald), famous illustrators (J.C. Leyendecker) and even famous photographers (Edward Steichen) had made substantial sums of money from magazine work. They treated such work seriously and actively sought it out. For Modotti there was the added element of politics as many of the magazines she worked for did not pay at all (*New Masses*) but had the leftist credentials that made them worth her time. While Weston had no such inclinations he also at times would publish in magazines published by friends (*Irradiador)* that could only afford token amounts. In any case both Weston and Modotti were published regularly all through their later stay in Mexico and even after they both went their separate ways and left the country as friends like Frances Toor and Anita Brenner kept publishing their work.

While Weston participated in the magazine *Irradiador* Modotti became a contributor to *Horizonte* in 1927 illustrating Marxist texts. While *Irradiador* focused on literature, art and politics *Horizonte* reversed the order of importance putting radical politics at the top. Rivera and Rufino Tamayo were regular contributors to the monthly magazine. While also a sounding board for Stridentist ideas *Horizonte* was more international, edited by the German poet List Arzubide. The magazine would collect poems by Federico García Lorca along with photos by Weston, Agustin Jiménez and Modotti. Photos in *Horizonte* did not illustrate text but were considered independent works of art. In his history of the Stridentist movement Arzubide included Modotti's *Lineas Telefonicas* as an example of "Stridentist aesthetics."

Modotti was also associated with *Mexican Folkways,* published by Frances Toor, the anthropologist and art historian. Toor studied indigenous cultures as an anthropologist and started *Mexican Folkways* in 1925 to act as a bridge between academic anthropology and essays aimed at the general public. They published Tina's short one page essay on photography, *Sobre la Fotografia* in December of 1929, the same year she had her one-person exhibition of photographs at the library at the University of Mexico – the essay was accompanied by her photo *Woman of Tehuantepec (Carrying a Jicapexle)* from 1929.

An article entitled "A Child Is Born in Tepoztlán" by the anthropologist Margaret Park Redfield was illustrated by Modotti with two portraits of the writer Luz Jiménez and her small daughter Conchita being breastfed. *Aztec Mother* (1926) and *An Aztec Baby* (1926) are eye level, frontal and sharp photographs. Nevertheless, her formalist tendencies show in her delicate framing. In the two-shot of Luz and Conchita looking straight at the camera Modotti shifts her framing to the right placing Luz's head on the left-hand edge of the frame creating a certain tension as the texture on the back wall now becomes a motif that plays off the hair and the clothing. In the breastfeeding shot the head of the baby and the breast are of equal size splitting the image into two halves with the ovals of head/breast meeting at the nipple of the mother that Modotti places in the center. Since "effects" of any sort were off-limits due to her own criteria of "good photography" framing was the one area that she was free to explore at length and she took full advantage.

Forma: Revista de Artes Plasticas (*Form: a Magazine of the Visual Arts*) was started in 1926 and also featured Modotti's *Cables Telegraficos, Tanque No. 1* and a series of photographs of workers. Her photos were also used to illustrate the murals of Orozco and Rivera in different issues. While *Forma* was more traditional and featured mostly painters and poets associated with the Mexican Renaissance it was sponsored by the Ministry of Public Education and the University of Mexico so had enormous prestige. She also took extensive photos of Orozco working, on a well-paid commission for the same magazine where the feature ran as a photo-essay on the construction of a mural.

Modotti also worked in 1926 with the magazine *30–30!* The radical journal received that strange name from the kind of rifle most used during the Mexican Revolution, the 30–30 carbine. As the title implies the magazine was hardline Communist and they used her photograph *Sombrero, Hammer & Sickle* (1927). The first issue even had an article by Martí Casanovas about her work entitled *"Las Fotos de Tina Modotti: El Anecdotismo Revolucionario"* ("Photos by Tina Modotti: Revolutionary Storytelling") which argued for an art that was pedagogical and illustrative – a requirement in Stalinist circles – while maintaining an "aesthetic sensitivity" that would be secondary but still present. For Casanovas many people could use photography to make art (Weston) or to make illustrations (Hugo Brehme) but only Modotti could do both.

Modotti also worked for *New Masses,* another Marxist-leaning magazine of the period, thanks to the American writer John Dos Passos who was a regular contributor and an admirer of Modotti's work. Dos Passos at that time was a Communist and, along with many "fellow travelers," seems to have seen Mexico as a baby step toward a worldwide Marxist revolution that would eliminate the class system, bringing forth a new era of peace, egalitarianism and brotherhood. While clearly this revolution was not meant to be, the idealism and camaraderie is palpable in the writing, art and photography of the period and the magazines reflected that communal spirit.

Throughout 1926 Modotti's photography started to receive as much exposure and recognition as Weston's. Weston himself acknowledged it and had no problems with Modotti's rising status and her newfound popularity; on the contrary he was proud of her and said so on various occasions. That same year she and Weston were in a group show at the Galeria de Arte Moderno along with drawings by Rivera and paintings by Charlot among others. The show was reviewed by Jorge Cuesta de Rafael and Vera de Córdova. The latter wrote: "Tina Modotti. Painters dream of someday making a work of art that could evoke as much emotion as these photographs by this most modern and vibrant of artists!" The high-octane prose, light on details, was typical of the period but one gets a sense that Modotti was now seen by the press as a master photographer.

Modotti also published her work regularly in *El Machete* and *Labor Defender,* taking pictures of May Day demonstrations in 1926. She also translated articles from Italian to Spanish, eventually pulling together a handful of progressive Italian expatriates to form the Anti-Fascist League of Mexico. But her most committed and long-lasting affiliation with a progressive political agenda was her membership in International Red Aid, an organization created by the Communist International that provided relief and first aid to thousands of Communists and "non-partisan revolutionaries" worldwide. The organization was also a front for Soviet propaganda and clandestine work. By 1927 Modotti was completely aligned with a Marxist program to which she was devoting large parts of her time. But by then Weston had already returned to California charting a new course for his work very different from Modotti's. Let's take a look at that break.

Edward as Tina and Tina as Edward

Their breakup begins with a reunion in Guadalajara in September 1925 provided by the city's Jalisco State Museum. The event was a two-person show of Weston and Modotti's Mexican pictures, organized by the artist Carlos Orozco Romero – their only two-person show in their lifetimes. The only review of the work by José Maria Peña talks more about the photographers than the work as they were already a well-known couple in Mexico by 1925 – "Edward and Tina" were an item.

Peña talks about being afraid that Modotti might be a "suffragette" from her way of dressing (plain and to the point) but goes on to say he was "pleasantly surprised by her sweet voice" and an appearance that was "very feminine." While surely this femininity must have been a relief to Peña one wonders how Modotti's acting skills came into play during her interview with the overly sensitive journalist. The author describes her face in great detail, noting that she smokes, but he barely mentions Weston except to say that he is a famous American, and he only describes the exhibition as "magnificent" without explaining why it is so.[62] Only six prints sold, which was a great disappointment to them as they were both in need of cash and were hopeful that the enthusiasm for their work would translate into sales. Weston had come with his teenage son Brett from California. His wife Flora, who, knowing or guessing about Weston's various affairs, including his open relationship with Tina, was scaling back her financial support to force Weston to return to the US.

Despite this setback Orozco Romero held a masquerade party in their honor "where they stylishly pulled off their usual stunt of exchanging clothes."[63] This "exchange" was not only a game of crossdressing it was a routine they both loved to perform at parties where each imitated the mannerism and personality of the other. After a few drinks Weston, wearing a plain gray dress in the style of Modotti, would shamelessly flirt with the men, while Modotti, wearing a conservative suit favored by Weston, would chat up the women complimenting them on their beauty with an exaggerated American English, making the women swoon in a haze of delight and laughter. The highlight was when they would both dance to contemporary jazz tunes. Tina was, of course, a talented actress and dancer – despite the fact that, strangely, she didn't like dancing – but apparently Weston, when prompted, was an outrageous exhibitionist and an excellent dancer. Perhaps he got that from his mother who was an actress, a performer who had forgone her work in the theater to raise a family.

In his *Daybooks* from 1944 that Weston attempted to destroy he beautifully recounts one of his evenings at Rivera and Lupe Marín's house party – it's a magnificent and invaluable piece of writing and one wonders why he would want to destroy it. Weston:

> We arrived at the party and Tina kisses Diego on the lips. It is a costume party and Tina is dressed as Edward Weston, mustache and all, and I am dressed as Tina Modotti, skirt, high heels, lipstick. Diego is our host and is dressed, characteristically enough, as himself. Diego accepts the kiss and gives me a wink, then walks into the living room arm in arm with Tina. "May I present you ladies and gentlemen, the great American photographer Edward Weston," he says, introducing Tina. Everyone bows and greets her cordially shaking her hand very gentleman-like. It is all very ridiculous but Tina plays the part rather well, looking a bit obtuse, sternly shaking men's hands, chivalrously kissing the ladies. I try my best to play my part but fumble around terribly in the heels. Marín seeing my distress comes and takes me by the arm and helps me along into the kitchen behind Diego and Tina... Diego calls out to Lupe, "Look Edward is here. Look how his hair is thickening – he runs his obese hands over her head as if he were petting a supine cat. Lupe in turn gives him a stern look, confirming my suspicions. "And who is this?" She says, pointing to me with

> one hand while she wipes the other on her apron. "His friend's whore?" Lupe storms out of the room. Diego follows upstairs where they proceed to scream at one another. Tina looks at me as Tina now, entirely herself. She unties the ribbon at the back of her hair and lets it down. She comes to me and places a hand on my stomach. I reach for the wig on my head but decide it's best not to bother."[64]

This extraordinary scene – typical of the fights that would eventually force Lupe Marín and Rivera to divorce – tells us that Weston was aware of Modotti's affair with Rivera without Tina having confessed to it, but regardless of that the love shown between Modotti and Weston here is extraordinary, profound and *quiet*. Neither of them needed the center stage spotlight or the exhibitionist histrionics typical of Rivera and his "family," as he called his close friends and lovers – they were all a highly dramatic, high-octane group that must have been entertainment enough for any evening. More importantly here the fact that Weston and Modotti could make fun of each other in such an open way at parties mimicking each other – in some sense also acknowledging that their work was now very similar – shows that both of them were strong personalities with a secure sense of self, even if they expressed doubts and frustrations in their letters and in Weston's *Daybooks*.

First and Second Class

On their return from Guadalajara to Mexico City Edward and Brett went first-class and Tina adamantly refused to travel in that "bourgeois" manner and went second-class. Weston recounts it in his *Daybooks*:

> Tina insisted on riding second class the journey to Mexico [City]. Brett and I had our first-class tickets straight through from LA so I bought a berth for Brett – too cruel to make such a sleepy head sit up all night, I thought, and I spent the night alternating between a watch over my cameras in first class and Tina in second, in the dim light among the Indians, sprawled over each other on the hard seats, dozing or drunken or garrulous.[65]

This scene of Weston "shuttling" between first and second class thanks to Modotti's class consciousness would have made a fine scene in one of the melodramas that Tina participated in while she was an actress in Hollywood. It also points to the more permanent separation soon to come.

Patricia Albers nicely sums up this break:

> Tina's act of class solidarity rankled Edward. Repelled by the Mexican militant's quasi-religious zeal and believing individualism the stance best suited to the artist, he took a dim view of his companion's newfound activism. She was not the same person to whom he had bid farewell in December, and if her insistence on sexual freedom was a barrier then, politics put a nearly insurmountable wall between them now.[66]

Weston was throughout his life apolitical, finding politics boring and history irrelevant – "yesterday's news" as the Americans used to say in Weston's day. While he readily admitted that he found Modotti's leftist politics and her feminist independence off-putting he was unable to see what now seems rather obvious, and that was that he was inside of history – in one of its most dramatic moments – without being conscious of it. Modotti was not only conscious but determined to make a difference. Something else that is clear is that Weston was jealous of Modotti's many admirers and lovers. Rumors were rampant and persist to this day, but he could not articulate his feelings in a meaningful way except to get angry and withdraw. A separation at that juncture was almost inevitable.

Glasses and *Casa De Vecindad*

Weston and Modotti not only cross-dressed and acted like each other for fun, there was a point at which they each took on the photographic practice of the other, and not surprisingly, they both excelled at it, matching each other point for point. Modotti's *Glasses* (1924–1926) is one of the masterpieces of Modernist formalist photography using the transparency and reflective surfaces to create a magnificent symphony of lights and darks across the surface of the print as the multiple ovals of the glasses seen at an angle create ellipses that intersect rhythmically in playful visual counterpoint in a field of black – the darkness here can't help but remind us of *My New Lover,* the marionette caught by its own shadow. It's almost as if she's riffing on Weston's brand of formalism, like a jazz singer, but doing it as well as the master. Something important to consider here is that Modotti has double-exposed the image to increase the number of glasses and create a sense of ambiguity and mystery in the intersecting and interpenetrating ellipses. This is something that Weston would never have done. This is the only surviving work by Modotti where she takes on the more avant-garde Modernist techniques that were being adopted as a matter of course by

Man Ray, Alexander Rodchenko, László Moholy-Nagy and the photographers of the New Vision. All of her other work in that vein – one-of-a-kind experiments in the camera or the darkroom – are lost.

Weston's *Casa de Vecindad II* (1926) is a strict social realist picture of the inner courtyard of a working-class apartment complex. The yard is full of white sheets hanging creating a repeating formal motif, but the emphasis is also on the people at work – women laboring on the stairs and a man leaning over to pick up some tools. The picture lacks a central focus that is a lesson learned from Stieglitz's *Steerage*. While its formal qualities are up front the picture has the clear social awareness of Modotti's Communist work. Weston and Modotti here change clothing, photographically speaking. Even in the titles Modotti uses the English and Weston the Spanish – it is a brilliant display by both artists but also, unfortunately, the last time they would trade lines in a photographic duet. Their photographic partnership was coming to an end, but that end was full of fireworks and brilliance.

The End: *Maguey Cactus* and *Workers Parade*

Weston's *Maguey Cactus, Mexico* and Modotti's *Workers Parade,* two pictures from 1926, are textbook examples of work that is Modernist but there is a major difference, and that difference is politics. The cactus in *Maguey Cactus, Mexico* takes up the whole frame conforming to Weston's new monumental style. The maguey is one of the many giant cacti that populate the landscape of Mexico, but in this case the plant's dark silhouette seems slightly threatening, a life force reaching out toward the cloudy sky, barely contained by the careful framing. *Maguey Cactus* articulates his fascination and fear of nature in a shot that is a beautiful formal interplay of sensual arabesques and folds. The reciprocity between the somewhat intimidating qualities of the cactus and the formal landscape play beautifully off each other – Weston's sensitivity here is extraordinary. By now he knows he is leaving Mexico soon, probably never to return, and he gives all of his pictures from this period a sense of farewell. Nevertheless, the picture is apolitical because its focus, literally and figuratively, is nature. Weston used all of his skills to focus on something ordinary and ahistorical and turn it into something extraordinary and magical. Giorgio Agamben nicely summed up the connection between metaphysics and nature: "Landscape is the house of Being."[67]

In *Workers Parade, 1926,* Modotti forgoes the sharp focus that Weston favors, but her work, shot from far above looking down, as if flying over the large group, charges the image with history and politics as if it had been hit by lightning. The workers, all wearing similar hats move as one solid mass. How did Modotti do it? Is it simply a matter of a different subject matter – cactus and workers – that makes the point? No, and the reason is that workers and poor people are sometimes photographed in a neutral or even a negative light – as in the Fascist photojournalism of the 1930s – therefore to simply depict them does not designate a leftist political perspective.

While the cactus and the workers are both obsessively framed Modotti focuses on people. They are a collective that is thinking and dressing as one, and while the photographer is above them she also brings the full weight of what anthropologists call "close observation" in their studies of unfamiliar peoples and cultures. Modotti took the photograph from Pablo O'Higgins's *azotea,* with Weston also present, as they watched the May Day celebrations below. Jorge Louis Borges liked to say that history is sometimes modest and likes to conceal its significant episodes. Modotti here sets out to expose history being modest as her photograph fully anticipates the fractious and epic mass struggles of the 1930s soon to come.

Modotti's picture seems to be hesitating – she doesn't get too close, maybe she even backs off. It's the extraordinary vulnerability and the unresolved emotional contradictions that make the shot, and that charges the picture with a subtle but powerful force. Modotti is emotionally and imaginatively with those people – she wants to share in their camaraderie and enthusiasm – but she is also at a remove, a formalist playing with the repeating oval shapes of the straw hats. In *Workers Parade* History comes to the fore and takes center stage – the political is aggressively up-front, take it or leave it. The picture is many things: a documentary portrait of a May Day protest, a manifesto, a cautious greeting to comrades, and a farewell to the art-for-art's-sake aesthetic of formalism. Significantly Weston was also on the roof that day but chose not to take any pictures.

A few months after that May Day parade Weston, along with his son Brett, traveled – by first-class train – from Mexico City to Los Angeles and never returned. Weston and Modotti's time together was brief but then so are many partnerships in art that produce great work – one need only look at Picasso and Braque who worked together seven years but in that period reinvented art for a new century. "Edward and Tina" explored the new 20th century, in Los

Angeles and Mexico City, using their cameras as art and ethnographic tools, exploring their time and place, but also, being artists, they used the medium to play, to challenge and to delight one another. Their partnership pushed them to produce their best and most innovative work that would not have been possible without the other.

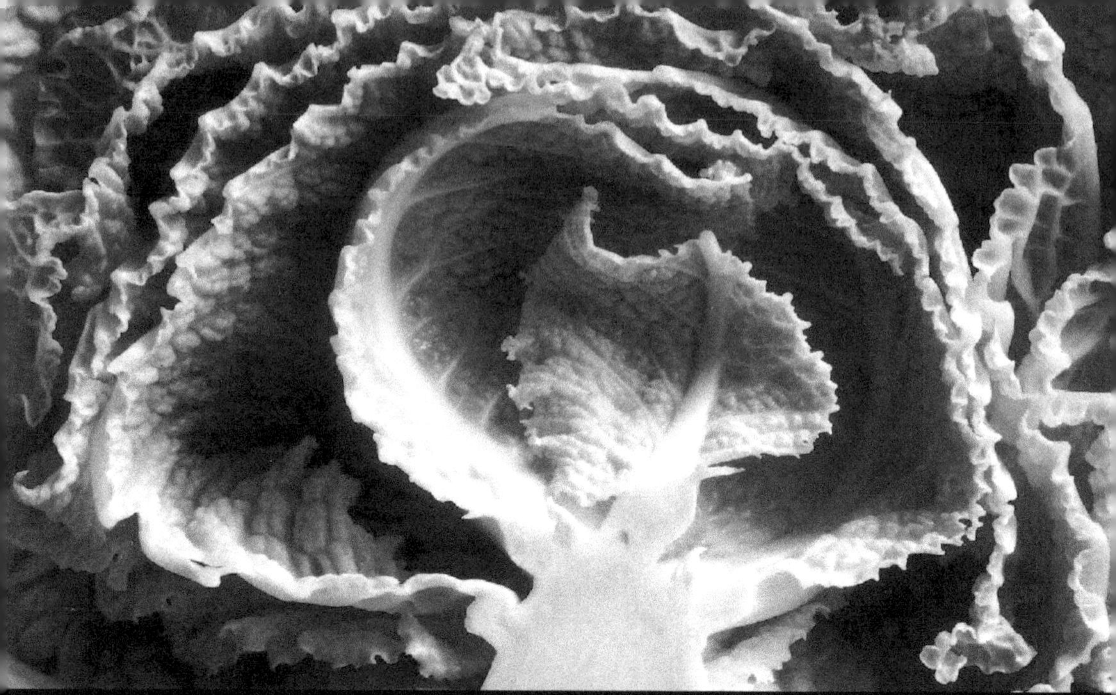

We were together. I forget the rest.

Walt Whitman, *Leaves of Grass*

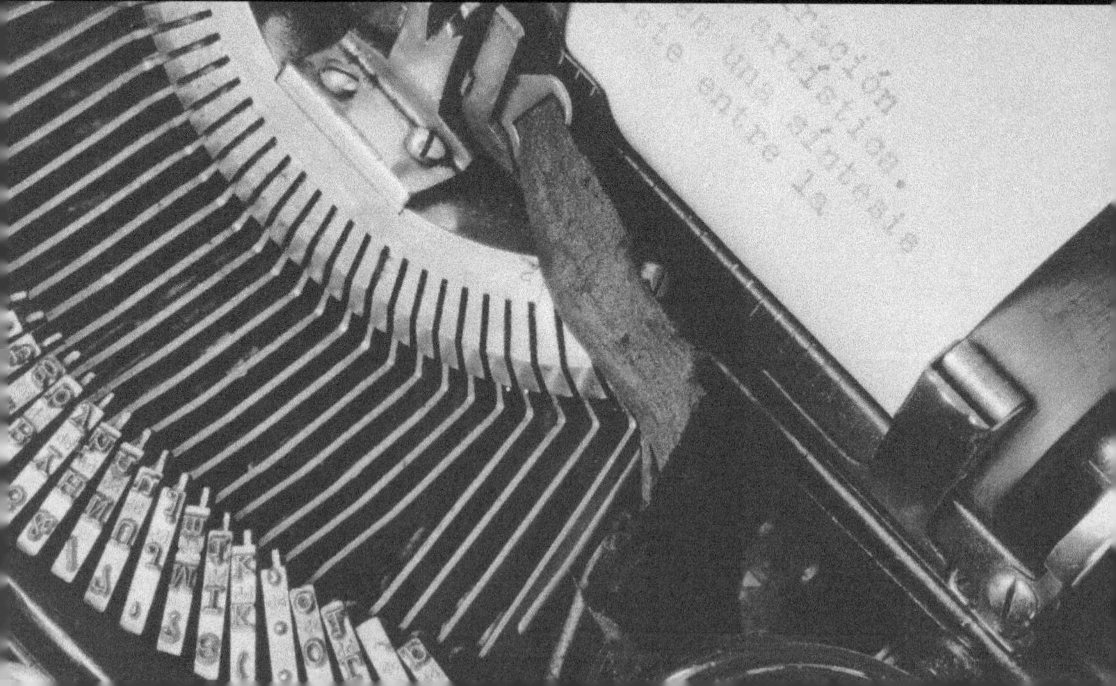

08

Weston's Leaves of Grass

I'll Tell You Later

From Weston's *Daybooks*, December 28, 1926:

> We faced each other speechless at the parting – hand clasp – tear filled eyes – a last kiss – Jean [Charlot] came to the station though I had warned him not to. Of course Elisa we brought with us, dear Elisa, pathetic little figure in black, and she cried too, indeed has wept by spells for two weeks past. I lay in a half stupor all day – emotional exhaustion, the shock of parting, worry and work…I seemed to realize that I was leaving not only Tina but dear friends and the land of my adoption too. Of course, I record a new pulqueria – *Despues te Digo – I'll Tell You Later.*[68]

Upon Weston's return to Los Angeles he arranged for an exhibition of his Mexican work at the University of California at Los Angeles where Americans, for the first time, saw prints of Weston's work made individually and alongside Modotti, as well as his active collaborations with her in the portraits/nudes and the *Idols Behind Altars* project. The exhibition was a revelation and Weston moved to the forefront of American photographers, not only amongst his peers but also to the wider cultural community.

Charis Wilson

That same year he started to photograph nudes again but in a much more conventionally classical manner, in the style of *Anita (Nude Back,* 1925) treating the naked body as an arena for formalist studies. This was a style then much favored by art institutions, including MoMA, so Weston had a powerful sponsor. He took up photographing nature, but never returned to the work of his

"Mexican period" for inspiration or subject matter. That highly complex interplay between formal play and improvisation, aestheticism and a snapshot aesthetic that he achieved with Modotti was not seen again.

In 1929 he met Sonya Noskowiak, a German-American photographer who became his muse, model, pupil and assistant in a pattern he would continue while married to Chandler from whom he had separated. But with Noskowiak, despite the fact that she was a photographer, Weston did not achieve a reciprocal relationship of equals – he was always the master and Noskowiak was always the "muse."

In 1934, at the age of 48, he met 19-year-old Charis Wilson who was the first woman, since his wife, who had no interest in being a photographer and, aside from modeling for him, spent her time writing about, promoting and selling Weston's work with success. Weston at one point asked Noskowiak to move out referring to women as "tides" that come in and go out.[69] For Noskowiak, who was emotionally devastated, being referred to as a "tide" might have only added insult to injury. In any case Wilson moved in and became Weston's new "muse" providing him with several bodies of work over a span of years.

Interestingly the nudes that he did of Wilson, that are now considered masterpieces of American photography, were taken in the Sierra Nevada Mountains, Point Lobos, Big Sur, Carmel and Santa Fe but in every case it is impossible to tell where one is – Charis is simply a "female form" in nature or in an architectural setting that was only used as a play of forms in space. Wilson was never individualized as he did with his portrait/nudes of Modotti.

In some of these outings into nature he was accompanied by Ansel Adams – Weston was an enormous influence on Adams's work and they shared a love of hiking, the outdoors, and photographing the female nude. Both men photographed Charis and Adams took informal photos with his Contax 35mm camera of the three of them on outings. These pictures have a greater sense of presence, of place, than his formal work, but he would have considered them mere snapshots. The pictures also beautifully capture the threesome's emotional bond and love of photography. Both men sought out idealized forms – whether female nudes or trees – not created (as a painter would do) but found in the world of reality, in the thing-itself, and then transformed by the artist-photographer into a two-dimensional plane of black and white.

The photographs taken of Charis at the sand dunes in Oceano, California, just north of Santa Barbara, in 1936 are considered by many photo historians the high point of his career. They show Wilson posing to create abstracted shapes with the sensuous dunes playing off Wilson's body in a musical play of forms. In that sense Weston seems to have returned to the lessons he learned as a Pictorialist and James McNeill Whistler's feeling for art as a form of visual music, but fusing that sensibility with the sharp focus and hard edges of formalism.

Group f/64

In 1932 alongside Adams and Imogen Cunningham Weston joined *Group f/64,* a collective of West Coast photographers named after the smallest aperture in the large format cameras they used. An aperture of f/64 gives you a wide depth of field and pinpoint focus. Its only drawback is that very limited light enters the camera so longer exposure times are often necessary. Their aim, expressed in essays, manifestos and exhibitions, was to champion "straight photography," which they defined as "possessing no qualities of technique, composition or ideas, derivative of any other art form."[70] There would be no painterly effects either toward realism or abstraction but only to photography itself. Nevertheless, Weston's imagination and intuitive drive could never be merely contained by labels or movements and he consistently absorbed Modernist motifs fully outside the ethos of "straight photography."

In 1938 Weston moved to a wooden cabin on Wildcat Hill in Carmel, California, near Point Lobo, a stretch of coastline that is a natural preserve south of San Francisco where he remained, on and off, for the remainder of his life. He photographed extensively there making Point Lobos his own preserve, as Adams made Yosemite National Park, and William Klein made New York City.

Weston and Charis in Santa Monica

Charis Wilson was not simply a "muse" but also a writer who wrote the text to various catalogs for Weton's shows, including *California and the West,* one of the classic American photo books. In perhaps the best known of these Weston/ Wilson collaborations – reproduced in posters and postcards – *Nude (Charis, Santa Monica)* from 1936, Wilson sits on the floor over a blanket as she hunches up, her arms across her legs forming a circle. Unlike the Modotti nudes/ portraits we don't see Wilson's face but only the top of her head as the hard Los

Angeles light pours down – the photo historian Nancy Newhall wrote that in this image Weston was using "light like a chisel."[71] The print needed a lot of work in the darkroom as the harsh, almost graphic contrasts of LA light had to be scaled back in the printing so they would not stand out as features, leaving the image less dramatic but more traditionally composed, its tones closer together and more temperate, more classical.

Weston had moved temporarily to Santa Monica, which was then a sleepy, inexpensive retirement community full of homeless people, used bookshops, and thrift stores. Due to the Depression his finances had taken a hit as the stock market crash of 1929 had wiped out his wife Flora's savings. He continued taking photographs of Wilson throughout the 1930s regardless of his financial situation but with four sons to support he was always looking for income. In 1937 Weston became the first photographer to receive a Guggenheim Fellowship and that gave him the opportunity to buy a car, travel the country to take pictures over a span of two years and divorce Flora – they had been living apart for 16 years.

Edward Weston & Walt Whitman

Weston and Wilson had married happily in 1939. Two years later Weston got the job of illustrating a new edition of Walt Whitman's *Leaves of Grass* – a great idea as Whitman was a poet of the everyday, the familiar, the overlooked. No other poet would have better understood Weston's *Escusado.* The Limited Edition Book Club edition was to be in two volumes and printed to the highest standards. Unfortunately, the editors made some predictable but unfortunate design choices that dimmed Weston's original vision. The pictures he took on the road were arguably his best body of work after his Mexican period. Weston's idea was original and to an extent even radical, paving the way for later excursions by the members of the Beat generation, most famously Robert Frank's *The Americans* (1958) with a memorable introduction by Jack Kerouac, and later Stephen Shore's classic book *Uncommon Places* (1982), where he uses a large format camera for a body of work that also owes a debt to Weston's *Leaves of Grass.*

While Whitman had been generally positive, even upbeat about the "Democratic Vistas" of America singing the hymns of the "body electric" and even speaking of himself as "containing multitudes," Weston took a different approach. He decided that rather than illustrate certain passages, as was then (and now) the norm, he would create his own visual photographic poetry to play off Whitman's text from 1855. In effect he would perform a duet with Whitman's poetry – two voices – as he had before with Modotti, turning the text into a ground or a *field* for a collage of image/text.

The pictures that Weston got are certainly not positive, upbeat or triumphalist as Weston shows rather a country just barely getting over the Depression, a wasteland of worn surfaces and everyday things discarded on the road to somewhere else. Weston's vision is almost postapocalyptic in many ways with empty urban spaces that look abandoned, but he retained the "plainspoken style" of straight photography, never veering toward surrealist juxtapositions and always letting the places and people speak for themselves.

His *Brooklyn Bridge* (1941) is probably still the best picture ever taken of this landmark New York structure. Weston radically decenters his frame with the most prominent part of the image taken up by Otto's Bar & Grill, a nearby restaurant. Clearly with *Brooklyn Bridge* Weston was looking to move beyond the narrow limitations of formalism, but he was also rejecting street photography, a photographic genre then coming into fashion. Rather, Weston was moving toward a cinematic approach that had, like his Mexican photos, a built-in mise-en-scène. But rather than choosing dramatic tableaux, as most cinematically inspired works tend to do, Weston chose the everyday aspect no one would notice, Otto's Bar & Grill. If *Brooklyn Bridge* were part of a traveling shot from the opening of a film it would not be the opening or the closing shot but the one in the middle, the in-between moment (again), but with fully American subject matter. This was a new direction for Weston.

His *Gulf Oil, Port Arthur, Texas* (1941) looks like a shot from a postwar science fiction film – perhaps a sequel to *War of the Worlds* (1953). A similar element of science fiction even permeates landscape shots such as *White Sands, New Mexico* (1941) as three flowering cacti crop up on sand dunes under a dark gray sky. The plants look extraterrestrial and the dunes are smartly dodged in the darkroom to create a flat overall field of light gray, almost white, eliminating all details. White Sands got its name because it is the world's largest area of gypsum sand in the world, which formed from an ancient, dried-up sea that existed 250–280 million years ago. Only the dunes in the foreground have sharp details serving as a stage to the main body of the image – a favorite Weston motif seen also in his Mexican pyramid photographs. This formal motif serves him beautifully here to create one of his most haunting and eerie late masterpieces.

Weston traveled to the places Whitman would have seen as he sought to help as a medic, or "wound dresser," during the American Civil War. His *Woodlawn Plantation House, Louisiana* (1941) shows a beat-up car in a decaying mansion built in the Neoclassical style. Weston plays off a young healthy tree on the left side of his frame to balance out the ruins giving a sense not only of lost time but of hubris getting its comeuppance as the stately columns from the mansion slowly sink into the earth of Louisiana. We are reminded here more of Shelley's *Ozymandias* than *Leaves of Grass* but Weston has made his point.

Of the 700 prints Weston made on his trip he wanted to use 90 with a full bleed. Charis Wilson also kept a log from the cross-country journey that would have served as an introduction. The editors rejected Wilson's log, chose 41 images from Weston's 90, placing them in a green, matted background, and made strict correspondences with quotes that gave his images an unintended illustrative aspect. The book was a commercial failure and Weston spoke publicly of being "disgusted" with it, but maintaining that the body of pictures from the trip was amongst his best work.[72] After the book fiasco he retreated to California to photograph landscapes and female nudes in an austere style, eliminating all extraneous elements in an attempt to achieve some sort of purity or essence – what he called in his *Daybooks* "the very substance and quintessence" of the thing itself. But as usual his work tended to transgress his own ideas – he shifted easily from formalist austerity, to homespun Americana, and from intimate minimalism to surrealist landscapes. An interesting example of the latter, using deep focus, is *Shell and Rock, Arrangement* (1931) that combines a small spider conch shell, looking like a white octopus, to a dark, almost blackened landscape, (actually Point Lobos), achieved in the darkroom, that might be another planet. Despite the small intimate size of the conch shell it dominates the geography as if it were a recently landed organic UFO – simultaneously pre and post historical. Like any great artist his work seemed to easily transcend whatever he or anyone else said about it.

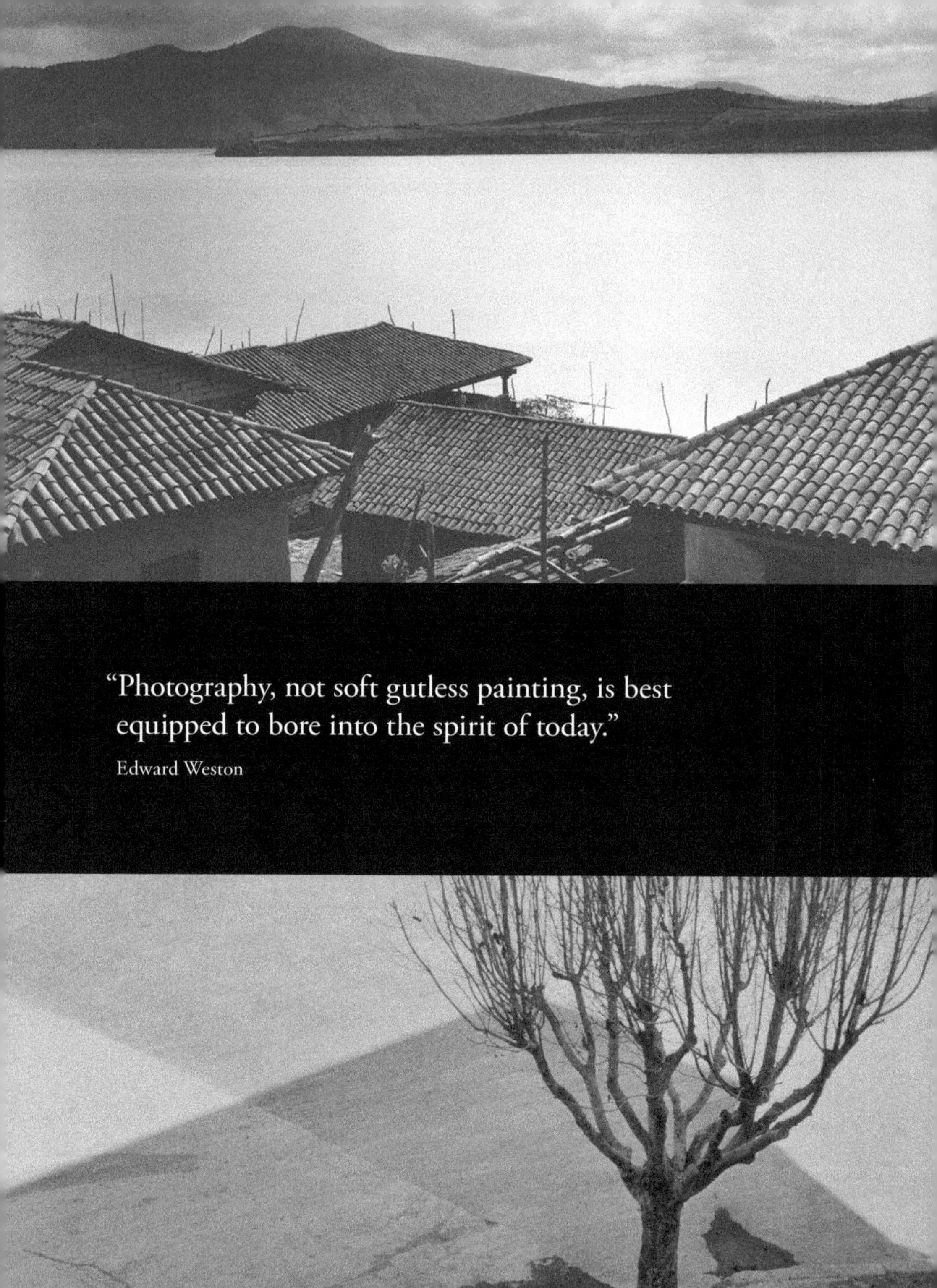

"Photography, not soft gutless painting, is best equipped to bore into the spirit of today."

Edward Weston

09

Weston Beach

Charis Floating

The best of these collaborations between Wilson and Weston is arguably a picture of Charis floating in her family's swimming pool at her father's 12-room house near Carmel – a conservative, upscale community on the Pacific coast south of San Francisco. The photo, from 1939, is titled *Floating Charis* and sometimes simply *Nude Floating*. The picture is a brilliant play of man-made Modernist forms and a nude – the odd-shaped, almost brutalist pool is made of cement in the rounded shape of a question mark with an enormous shallow step leading to a very dark and deep pool. Weston placed Wilson floating facing up directly in the middle of these two spaces, with her legs on the shallow step and the rest of her body floating on the deep side. Her hands are close to her pubic hair while her breasts and her face are the only parts of her body not underwater. Her eyes are mysteriously closed, turning the body into an odalisque. In the darkroom Weston smartly emphasizes the blackness of the deep water and uses it to play off against Charis's pale white skin.

Her closed eyes and body language suggest a corpse and the pool has an eerie aspect of modernism in ruins, as if she were floating on an abandoned site. With her body literally floating between shallow and deep waters the image also suggests a montage of sorts, a before and an after, but shrouded in stillness and mystery. While the image is not a portrait/nude, as was his work with Modotti, this cinematic aspect, that was a feature of his "Mexican period," had gone missing from his work since his return to California, but suddenly with this picture Weston seems to get some of that old fire back. Perhaps this had to do with the modernist location – maybe the house triggered something and he decided to use the cement pool as a thematic element. In any case the image is a brilliant collision of architectural formalist studies and nude that harkened back to his days with Modotti.

Charis in Reno Getting a Divorce

During the road trip to take pictures for *Leaves of Grass* Weston and Wilson began to drift apart as Wilson felt her writing was not appreciated – many of the books credited solely to him had in fact been co-productions with her doing the writing but Weston never spoke about her except as his "muse." He also continued to be fascinated by younger women as "muses" so as the years went by Charis was more isolated and more frustrated. Wilson was growing tired of it and in 1946 they divorced. Weston wrote to Beaumont Newhall, the photo historian and friend: "Charis in Reno getting a divorce. Cole [his son)] in LA getting a new Chevrolet." The line sounds like a poem or a song – very sad, very isolated, and very American.

In 1945 Weston was diagnosed with Parkinson's disease but in the initial stages it was slow in showing its effects and he continued working. The following year, at age 59, he had a retrospective at MoMA that emphasized his formalist credentials, at the expense of his more personal, idiosyncratic and adventurous works made in Mexico. This is a period that was treated as a "sowing of wild oats" – personally and photographically – before his more "mature" works. The classification of the work from his "Mexican period" that happened in subsequent years as "immature" was seen by cultural institutions as a form of purification where Weston, back in California, finally got down to essences. This simplistic and soporific institutional narrative chimed in with the postwar need to "return to order," to reconfigure classicism for a new era – the love of empires for classical art/architecture is well documented and in this area the US was no exception. The calm and orderly celebrations of nature and the human form that Weston produced after 1926 on a regular basis proved popular, extending his fame and sealing his reputation.

Due to health issues Weston was not able to travel for some years and stayed in his cabin in the woods near Point Lobos creating an extensive body of work. This is Sean O'Hagan: "Point Lobos is a beautifully elemental place that remains much as it was in Weston's time. It is a wild place that drew artists, photographers and film-makers long before Weston settled there…its angular rocks, tangled seaweed, bent cypress trees, sun-scorched driftwood – possess an almost unearthly beauty that is both austere and sensual, somehow not so 'heightened' through technique as his more famous pictures."[73]

In 1948 Weston took his final photograph at Point Lobos that he titled *Rocks and Pebbles, 1948* – he had gone from chickens on his aunt's farm in 1908 to pebbles and rocks in Point Lobos in forty years – in a sense the work circles back to its beginning but now the photo has the calmness, and the underlying multiple meanings typical of a master's late work. The picture has the purist formal qualities of an elegant abstraction and the practical literalness of a photo depicting one of the simplest geological formations on earth – the image captures "the very substance and quintessence" (his term) of the thing itself.

But the wily Weston also had a final ace up his sleeve – the clue is in the title *Rocks and Pebbles, 1948*. Pebbles are rocks that have been weathered by the movement of water, other rocks, and wind to their humble small size – a million years ago they might have been boulders the size of trucks and a million years in the future they might be part of the sandy sediment, the water, and even the salty air. If we know what we are looking at a pebble can tell us the stories of long dead stars, vanished continents, and warm oceans full of volcanic activity and strange creatures that we never got to know.

Weston's picture suggests these mysteries without unlocking their secrets or providing us with a scientific formula that might lead to a conclusion – he merely shows us this transition, this metamorphosis, from rocks to pebbles to air, as something both ordinary and extraordinary, quotidian and sublime. By incorporating the year 1948 as part of the title Weston places a marker in time, like a placard in the ring of a tree on display showing the various geological eras – it proclaims "I was here." As his own body was falling apart he must have seen not just the natural world but all of observable reality, even the mighty rocks, as fellow travelers in the long and complicated story of Nature – a story we are only now just barely beginning to understand.

As the Parkinson's disease progressed he was no longer physically able to use his cameras or do darkroom work. His final "muse" and assistant, Dody Weston Thompson (who married his son Brett), helped him catalog and print a selection from a lifetime's body of work – 830 8x10-inch prints. In 1950 he had another major retrospective at the Musee National d'Art Moderne in Paris with images printed by Dody and Brett. At the age of 71 Weston died on the first day of 1958. His sons scattered his ashes into the Pacific Ocean, an area of pristine sand and ocean near Point Lobos then known as Pebbly Beach but that was later renamed Weston Beach. Over the years this location has become a mecca of sorts for photographers and photo historians who visit yearly in search of "Edward Weston."

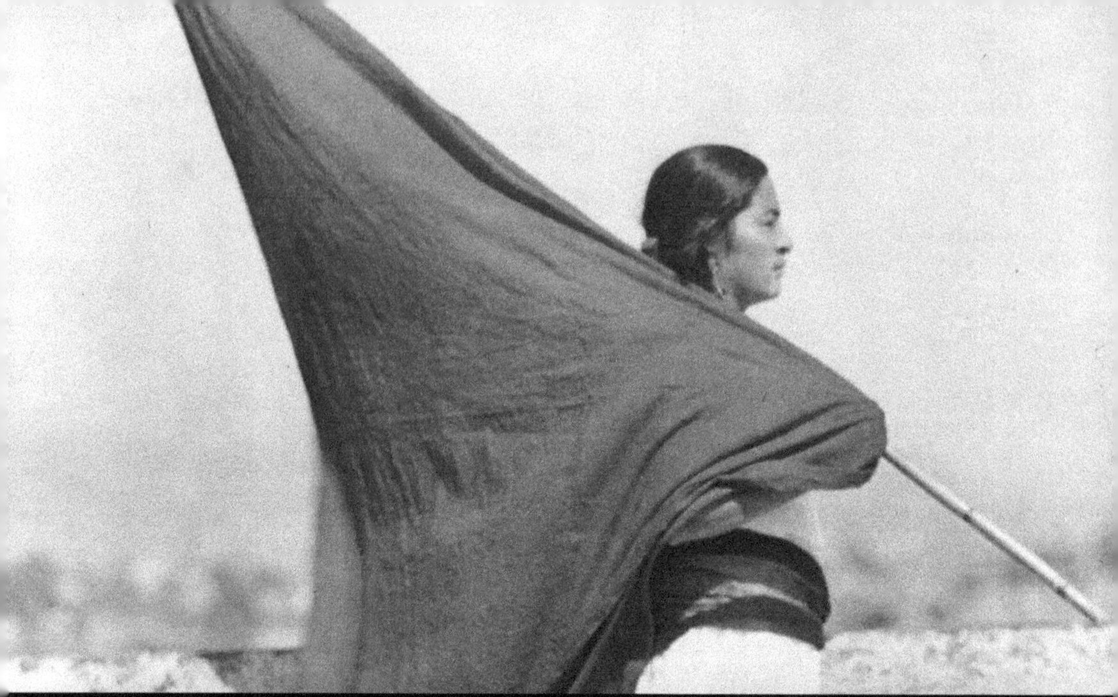

The ultimate end of all revolutionary social change is to establish the sanctity of human life, the dignity of man, the right of every human being to liberty and well-being.

Emma Goldman, *Nowhere at Home, Letters From Exile*

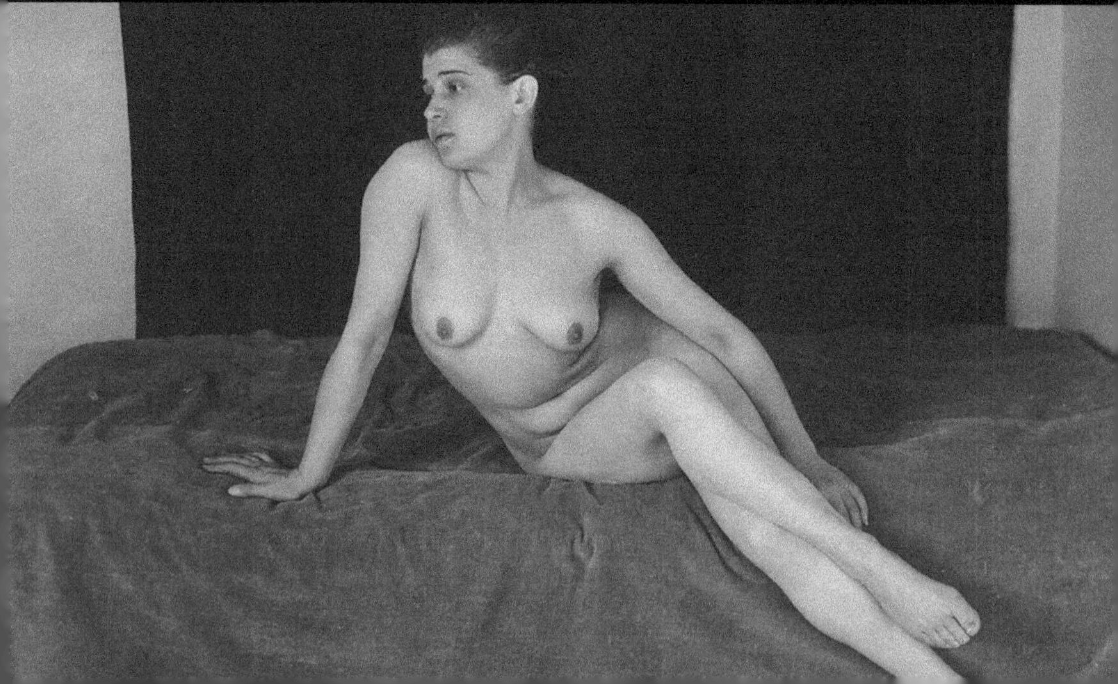

10

In the Arsenal: Mella & Tinisíma

Red Aid

The great Mexican photographer Manuel Álvarez Bravo, who had known Tina since he was a youth, categorized her career into two parts: "Romantic" and "Revolutionary." 1927 was the year when she made that transition, joining the Communist Party as well as starting a new relationship with Xavier Guerrero, a painter heavily involved in the muralist movement. For a time he lived in the same house as Rivera and Frida Kahlo, as did Leon Trotsky – Guerrero and Rivera worked side by side in mural work and in political efforts. He also co-founded *El Machete* along with David Alfaro Siqueiros in 1924. Unlike Weston Guerrero was not in any sense a challenge for Modotti as an artist, a lover, or a colleague – he was notoriously silent to the point that he was constantly teased about it but always seemed proudly melancholy and self-contained. Guerrero traveled to Moscow in 1927 for a long-term stay to receive training in propaganda and clandestine work signaling that he was on the side of Stalin, as was Modotti. The left was typically divided in the Twenties and after. These divisions reached a crescendo of self-destruction and recriminations during the Spanish Civil War (1936–1939) – the subject of George Orwell's scathing *Homage to Catalonia* (1938).

The most powerful groups within the factions inside the Communist cause were the Stalinists and the Trotskyites. Rivera and Kahlo sided with Trotsky and as a result Modotti felt it necessary to terminate her relationship with them. Rivera was officially thrown out of the Communist Party (controlled by Moscow) in 1929, the same year he married Frida Kahlo. But the politics within Mexico City on a day-to-day basis were ambiguous, confusing, ever-shifting, and dangerous.

A good example was Adelina Zendejas, a friend of Rivera, Kahlo, Modotti and their circle, had all of the credentials necessary to be not only a "leftist" but on the vanguard of feminism in Mexico. She had a doctorate in philosophy, putting herself through school by working in a restaurant; she was a teacher of history and director of La Escuela Taller Para Obreras Y Empleadas (School and Workshop for Workers and Servants); she wrote extensively for a variety of newspapers and journals on subjects ranging from the dangers of imperialism to children's rights. In short, her "left" credentials were impeccable. But Zendejas had no affiliation with either Stalin or Trotsky – could she be trusted? Everyone was friendly to her but cautious.

In the following year, 1928, Modotti started perhaps the most intense emotional and sexual relationship of her life with Julio Antonio Mella, an exiled Cuban Marxist and one of the founders of the Cuban Communist Party. Their meeting happened as they were both helping to organize demonstrations in Mexico City for Nicola Sacco and Bartolomeo Vanzetti. During the same organizational strategy meetings at Red Aid Modotti also met Vittorio Vidali, a fellow Italian exile whom she befriended. Vidali was a ranking member of Red Aid and had been to Moscow to receive training – like Modotti he had lived in various cities, was considered charming, cosmopolitan, and knew his way around.

Vidali would come to play a large role in Modotti's later life but at that moment they were working to free Sacco and Vanzetti, also Italian immigrants, who were anarchists controversially accused of murdering a guard in Braintree, Massachusetts, a conservative community in the US. The trial was clearly influenced by anti-Italian, anti-immigrant, and anti-anarchist sentiments then at their peak. Despite obvious problems with the trial – including retractions of confessions – the men were executed in 1927.

Mella was tall, athletic, charismatic and reckless. He had the ideological convictions of Trotsky, the oratorical skills of Fidel Castro, and the charm and good looks of Che Guevara – in short Mella was dangerous and carelessly courted hatred and envy. He wrote for a variety of leftist newspapers, including *Cuba Libre* and *El Machete,* for which Modotti sometimes provided photos. Both Modotti and Mella were, in a sense, self-invented people. While Assunta Adelaide Luigia was Tina's real name Mella's was Nicanor McPartland y Diez.

Mella had emigrated to the US and tried to enlist in the Army while still a teenager and was thrown out of the country – shades of Fidel Castro joining an open tryout with the Washington Senators, a major league baseball team then based in Washington DC. At the age of 17 Mella tried to join the Mexican Army but was refused for being a Cuban. He became a Communist and was, in 1925, accused of throwing bombs in a Havana theater box office, after which the Party expelled him – not for throwing a bomb but for having ties to the bourgeoisie. Lacking any road forward he decided to go to Mexico City and try his luck as word of the Mexican Renaissance was out. Many people, including Diego Rivera, had warned Mella and suggested that he get a bodyguard, something he refused to do. The vicious infighting within leftist circles was confusing even to them – explanations could sometimes last all night long and, typically, end inconclusively.

Let us try to summarize Mella's precarious position and why Rivera suggested a bodyguard. Mella was a Trotskyite and so an anti-Stalinist who wanted to overthrow Gerardo Machado, the right-wing hardline president of Cuba who was a close ally of American business interests that had heavy investments in Cuba. Trotsky took a hardline stand wanting Machado to leave or be overthrown. But the Cuban Communist Party, that took orders from Stalin, was seeking a "modus vivendi" between Machado and the Party where they might both share power. The Stalinists saw Machado, despite his macho posturing, as a lightweight who could eventually be forced from power into exile or be assassinated – appeasement with him was seen as a distasteful but necessary step on the road to power. Machado saw the Communists simply as dangerous scum that needed to be sidelined until he could figure out a way to get rid of them or, even better, have the Americans do it. In effect the Trotskyite Mella was the odd man out for both the Stalinist Communists and Machado's right-wing thugs in power – it is clear that even with a bodyguard Mella's days were perhaps numbered.

The love affair between Mella and Modotti was intense and subsumed other relationships. She thought she had finally found a replacement for the large hole left by the departure of Weston that seemed to only get larger and more imposing as time went on – instead of healing, the damage made by his absence was festering and she was becoming desperate. She wrote a long letter to Xavier Guerrero in Moscow to explain that she had found a new man and was deeply in love and wished him the best. The letter was clearly difficult to write as it is tortuously self-conflicted, guilt-ridden and apologetic. Guerrero's one-word reply was typically brief and to the point: "Adios."

While Mella was uninterested in photography or any of the arts – his one and only focus was politics – the physical relationship they developed in their short time together was intense and all encompassing. Here Elena Pianotowska in her novel *Tinísima* (Mella's nickname for her) recounts their relationship in her typically dramatic style:

> The first time that Tina and Julio were left alone in the offices of El Machete, her entire body became expectant, like a hunting dog, waiting in perfect tension. Tina sought to close her lips that opened involuntarily, to quiet the beating heart under her bellybutton. They made love standing up, then over the newspapers that had fallen on the floor. Neither of them worried that someone from El Machete would discover them. Forgetting herself Tina felt herself Julio. She was Julio, he was Tina, she was the desire of Julio and he felt the same. Tina looked at him and saw herself in his eyes, and behind him was the Tina that she aspired to be. "I want to be what I see behind your eyes, Julio, I want to be what you see." Julio provided her with access to a certain kind of knowledge, the best conception of herself.[74]

Poniatowska's overheated prose probably gets the passion and confusion of the moment better than any photographic study of Modotti's pictures from this period. Part of Mella's charm was that he assumed he was invincible and going to live forever – he could not dial down his outrage over capitalism's grotesque abuses or his enthusiasm for a new world to come under Trotsky. He attracted a wide variety of poets, revolutionaries, artists, students, and hangers-on. They met regularly in an open Chinese restaurant on Argentina Street in the center of the city where the restaurant's long tables were perfect for their marathon, raucous lunches – one wonders where they found the time.

Mella Becomes a Martyr

On January 10, 1929, Modotti and Mella were walking home at night to the Zamora building, "a multi-story brick construction that was the haunt of bohemian writers, artists, and radicals."[75] Since leaving Weston, Modotti had pared down her lifestyle to more modest bohemian quarters where transients mixed with students, aspiring artists, and writers. Mella had been warned earlier that day by José Magriñat, a fellow Cuban exile, that Machado had sent assassins from Cuba to kill him but there was no way to know how accurate this information was. Mella decided to go home but just as the couple almost reached the Zamora building a gunman came out of the darkness, fired two shots and killed Mella. Tina claimed to have felt the bullet graze her and smelled it but she was unhurt.

Modotti was questioned repeatedly as she was a prime suspect in the killing despite the fact that it was her lover who was the victim. Police ransacked her apartment and Modotti, as was typical of Communists at that time, had her small space full of Marxist posters, books and party slogans written on the walls with paint. Mella became a martyr to the Communist cause before the blood on the streets was dry. He even seems to have sensed that himself as he lay dying, he screamed out to tell the world that Machado and the Cuban secret police had killed him and he was dying for the revolution – the apocryphal story might sound like one of Modotti's Hollywood melodramas but it was corroborated by people nearby, especially one bystander who didn't see the murder but heard everything clearly.

Unfortunately for Modotti there were inconsistencies in the trial. First, she gave a false name to the police to protect her portrait photography business; secondly Mella was killed by a gun at point-blank range from the left side, while Modotti claimed to have been holding his left arm – how could she, as she claimed, have not seen the killer who must have been standing inches away from her? Lastly the letters from Guerrero to her from Moscow, were all signed X, creating a sense that the simple letters must be coded messages from Moscow, while in fact, Guerrero singed X because his first name was Xavier.

The newspapers predictably had a field day and squeezed every possible ounce of melodrama from the trial, treating Modotti like a femme fatale, using film stills from her days in Hollywood where she, in fact, played femmes fatales. They also showed nude photos taken by Weston that were sure to turn the conservative Catholic community against her. To make matters worse the police seemed to be colluding with the press to squeeze every possible ounce of attention possible from the murder but their motive is unclear – to stoke anti-Communist sentiment? Payoffs by the press to police were then a commonplace and possible, but inconclusive as there was no proof, just the familiar dog-and-pony show of the powerful elites and the press.

The police, headed by Valente Quintana, a rabid anti-communist, called in Dr. Maximilian Langsner, an American hypnotist with presumed telepathic powers, or "magnetic" powers as he called them, to assist in the case. Langsner was a character straight out of Fritz Lang's *Dr. Mabuse* films but had become famous and fashionable in Mexico not only by working with the police to solve crimes and get confessions under hypnosis, but by driving a Chrysler (an enormous American car) through the streets of Mexico City blindfolded. Dr. Langsner's remarkable feat notwithstanding his attempts to hypnotize Modotti and get a confession through hypnosis proved inconclusive. Nevertheless, the doctor insisted that he could sense it was a crime of passion and Modotti was guilty. Rivera wrote a letter attacking the police for turning the event into a circus, focusing only on Modotti, to appease the Cuban government – and by extension the Americans who kept Machado afloat with unlimited guns and money.

There were other Cuban exiles in Mexico City, principally José Magriñat, who was known as one of Machado's henchmen doing clandestine work, and living quite well, but the police didn't bother to question them, putting all of their chips on getting a confession from Modotti. The police also requested that Tina go to the site and re-create the scene of the murder at the exact hour that it happened, with news cameramen invited. In short order the police had managed to make Modotti the most famous and notorious woman in Mexico.

The tabloids developed different theories depending on the journal. They accused her of being secretly a fascist spy, or conversely of being a Stalinist agent who had played Mella and then killed him. The most plausible of the theories they developed was that Modotti was working – via Red Aid – as an undercover agent keeping track of Mella's activities but she fell in love with him. Once she realized that the Party was going to kill him she had to choose sides and she chose the Party. At least this last theory has the benefit that it takes into account the facts of the case and Modotti's psychological collapse after the killing – but there is no evidence to support it.

Tina's friends and colleagues came to her defense from Rivera down to the lowliest workers for Red Aid. The international women's group published a statement outraged that she was being vilified as a fascist killer when she was clearly neither. Carleton Beals and Rivera had to explain that the photos of Modotti nude were actually works of art by Edward Weston, not pornography, as apparently the police were not able to see the difference.

Finally, the police chief, Quintana, who was clearly obsessed with Modotti, was fired and a new investigation started. Within a few days of his sacking José Magriñat, the Cuban who had met Mella the night of the murder – the same man who told him to be careful – was arrested and charged with the crime but no clear evidence could link him to the murder. What was certain was that a gunman killed Mella, not Modotti, and that it was a political crime not one of passion. Conspiracy theories were many and persist to this day but nothing has ever been proven.

Modotti was cleared of the murder but the death of Mella and the subsequent investigation that had turned into a media circus all seem to have taken something out of her, as if she had died herself in the altercation but her body and brain still functioned more or less in the same fashion, so she decided to put it to some use for the Party. Mella in a sense called out the murderer himself as he lay dying – he had been warned that the plot to kill him was already underway and so it proved to be but it happened much faster than he or anyone imagined.

A year before the murder Rivera had portrayed Vidali, Modotti and Mella in his mural *In the Arsenal* housed in the Secretariat of the Public Education headquarters in Mexico City. The mural depicts the proletarian revolution to come with Frida Kahlo at the center handing out rifles to peasants – a highly unlikely event under any circumstances. He also included Tina, very stern and sad, holding a belt of ammunition while Vidali, hiding behind a wall, suspiciously stares over her shoulder wearing a black hat. Modotti gazes lovingly at Mella who takes the ammunition from Tina but looks off beyond her outside the mural to something we can't see – something that has caught his eye. The proletarian revolution never came but Rivera's insightful mural seems to capture the three players in an ambiguous drama, with Vidalli, Modotti and Mella in the middle of something beyond their control.

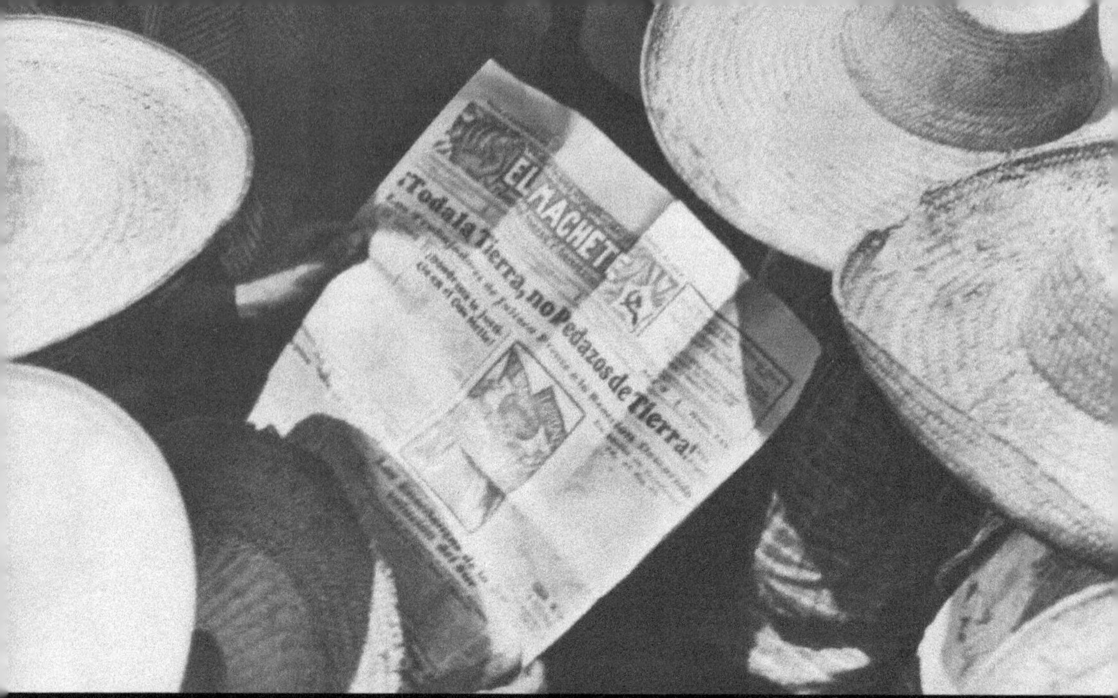

They are so damn 'intellectual' and rotten that I can't stand them anymore…I would rather sit on the floor of Toluca and sell tortillas than have anything to do with those artistic bitches in Paris.

Frida Kahlo, *Letters of Frida Kahlo*

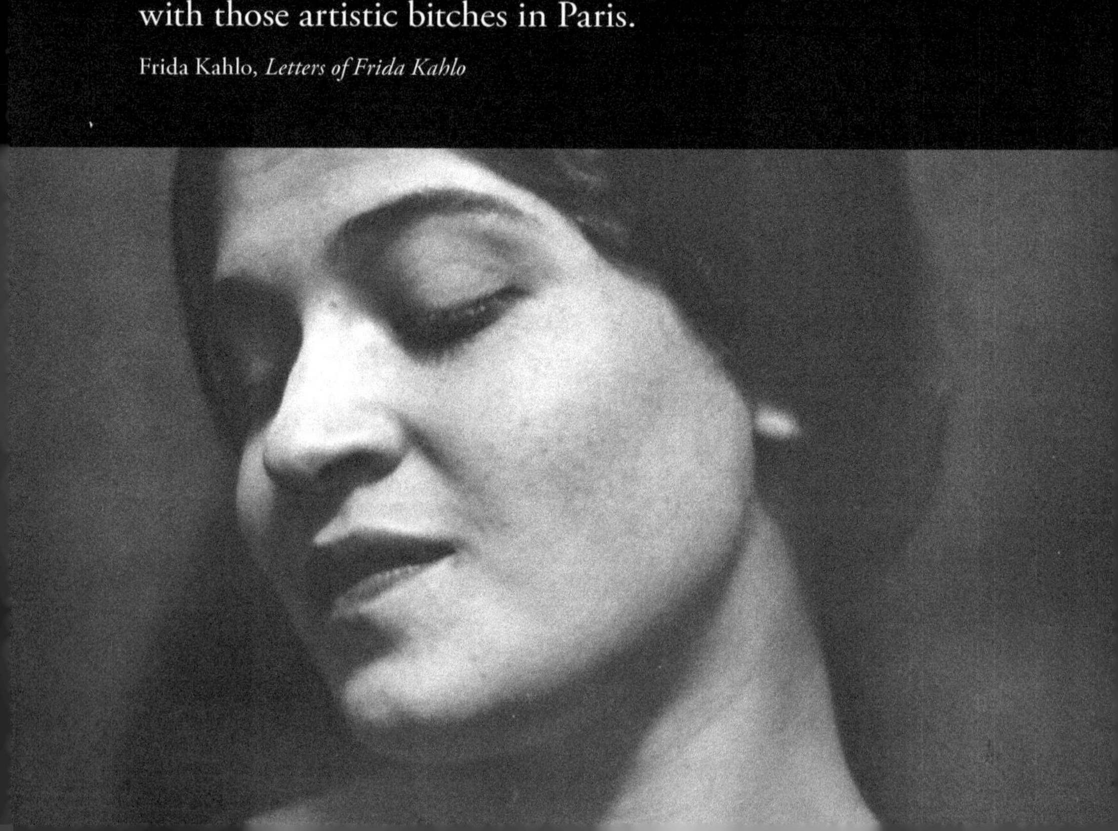

11

In Tehuantepec: A Greeting to Comrades

A Short Trip

Modotti by 1926 had moved to a bifurcation in her photography that seemed unresolved – whether she consciously set out to separate her work is not clear but seems unlikely since most artists don't approach their own body of work academically but instinctually. On the one hand with pictures like *Calla Lily* (1924–26) she had clearly reached a level of formalist mastery that equaled Weston's, or anyone then working in formalist photography in Europe. But she had another body of social documentary work, such as *Obreros, 1926* (*Workers, 1926*), that concentrated on the poor, the disenfranchised and their environment – we might call these her *indigenismo* pictures.

In the academic literature devoted to Modotti the Tehuantepec pictures are often referred to as "worker photographs" but this generic term has its drawbacks, principal among them is that it fails to take into account the obvious fact that Modotti was a Communist, and so photographing workers has a different meaning for her than when Lewis Hine or Margaret Bourke-White photographed workers building the New York City skyline we know today.

For Hine and Bourke-White the workers represented triumphalist progress at ground level, the nobility of work organized toward the building of an empire. For Modotti the worker – invariably an *indigeno* – represented an exploited class that would ultimately triumph over their masters, the oligarchy, through nobility, strength of character, and solidarity. As has been pointed out this body of work clearly anticipates the social documentary photography of the following decade personified in the US by the WPA, most obviously Dorothea Lange, who, like Modotti, concentrated on individuals, particularly women and families. But Modotti goes further than Lange by not only heroicizing her *indigenos* but searching for a *communality* with her fellow workers – her photographs are in a sense a greeting, or an open letter to comrades – something that American photographers never actively sought to do.

After the murder of Mella and the subsequent events with the police Modotti needed a break from the madness and theater of Mexico City. She decided to travel to Oaxaca and Tehuantepec. The region was well-known then and now for its women, known as *Tehuanas*, who have carved out a culture based around the marketplace – a strong matriarchy that has lasted centuries regardless of who rules Mexico at the moment. In fact, the *Tehuanas* have a certain contempt for the macho patriarchy that resides in Mexico City, with their fancy suits, big houses and American cars, seeing them as overgrown boys, lost and playing dangerous games they themselves don't seem able to control. They reasoned that when they are long gone and forgotten the *Tehuanas*, like the river and the mountains, would still be around making their extraordinary dinners and laughing at the *pinches cabrónes* in their suits.

The Mexico City intellectuals that would have spoken to Modotti about Tehuantepec made much of the Zapotec heritage, suggesting an authentic, anticolonial culture similar to *indigenismo* but without the overt political ideology or sloganeering. The distinctive dress of the women later became a rage among Mexico City intellectuals, eventually becoming Frida Kahlo's trademark style. These women seemed to be "naturally" radical within the context of Mexico – and the West generally – and artists and intellectuals gravitated to the area to, in a sense, receive inspiration.

Modotti's street photography and portraits from her trip have the aspect of snapshots but this is clearly a quality that she is imposing on the work as a motif as she was using a newly acquired Graflex camera where the snapshot element must be imposed willingly with some care. Tina had sold her Korona camera that Weston had given to her, that needed a tripod, and had exchanged it for a Graflex camera that is not only portable and relatively light but also easy to focus, and the film, in the form of cartridges, can be changed more quickly than a conventional large format camera so it can almost be handled like a 35mm.

Some of the work from Tehuantepec has been recognized by institutions, such as *Woman of Tehuantepec* (1929) and *Woman of Tehuantepec Carrying a Jicalpextle* (1929) as these photographs tend to fuse the "heroic worker" with Weston's brand of formalism, and so they are easy-to-read pictures and rather one-dimensional. They don't seem able to escape their propagandistic foundation while their formalism is paint-by-numbers. Regarding this series some writers, like Isabel Tejeda Martín, even put a stress on the established institutional feminist perspective: "Rather than conceiving the female body in a scopophilic way, as objects for visual pleasure, women were presented in Modotti's case as subjects who work, who participate in politics, who suffer and who care for their fellow humans beings."[76] The problem here is that this perspective assumes that, particularly with a male viewer, the scopophilic or voyeuristic approach and the perception of women as independent reasoning subjects are mutually exclusive – in fact they are not – the most we can say is that they might be so in some cases, or even most cases. Helpfully Modotti shatters that soporific illusion with this series and puts any attempt to turn her into a feminist *à la lettre* to pasture.

Other works from the same series that have not received much attention are much more interesting, more radical, precisely because they do not fit the parameters of either formalism, or heroic illustration that institutions are so fond of. Her *indigenismo* pictures are among her best work precisely for being so hard to pigeonhole. In *Woman From Tehuantepec Mexico* (1929) an older woman carrying a jicalpextle – a basket or container that usually carried groceries or water and rested on top of the head – stands on a large stone step with two classical columns behind her. The photo looks like it might have been taken 2,000 years ago somewhere in Mesopotamia or Greece. Modotti beautifully decenters her frame – pulling the leg of formalism one might say – by putting the women off to the left. The woman's shoulder just catches one of the columns that is in the middle of her frame. Strangely the sky and the stone steps are the same gray, creating a creepy sense of the ephemeral and the solid being one. She took several shots here so was looking for that correspondence of tones. It's one of her most stunning pictures and it is also completely Modotti owing nothing to anyone.

Another masterpiece from this series is *Two Tehuanas and a Pig* (1929) that shows a woman and a girl, probably her daughter, both carrying jicalpextles on their heads. The daughter holds hers with one hand not having mastered the balancing act yet while the mother easily balances hers. Their clothing is ancient and modern, the pig in the foreground and the fortress-like building in the background bracket the women. It's the closest that Modotti ever got to capturing a glimpse – the photograph has the effect of seeing something from a moving bus just before we pass by and it is gone forever. The big smiles of the women convey both a greeting and a farewell, a sense of solidarity – working women to working woman – that must have pleased Modotti greatly as she catches for a second that brief glimpse of glory when you connect with people you love – for that instant everything seems possible. If this photo were to have a music score it would certainly have to be *The Internationale* – the anthem of various anarchist, communist, socialist, and social democratic movements.

With *Basket Market Oaxaca* (1929) Modotti seems to again be teasing Weston and his brand of formalism. An outdoor stand selling baskets has a makeshift roof that puts the women selling their wares in darkness while the baskets are in the glaring, clean, intense light of the area. The repeating ovals of the baskets are pure Weston, but there behind the ovals, in the darkness, two women sit cautiously waiting to be acknowledged as if they had been there centuries. Modotti was a darkroom master by now and could have easily burned in the interior of the space so it would not be as dark and blended in with the baskets but she didn't; she lets the darkness and the high contrast do all the talking. The ethnographic intention (foreign to Weston) here is clear as Modotti is curious about the material and social culture of these women – clothing, crafts, habitat, etc., as well as their ceremonies and customs, but above all the underlying spirit of solidarity and communal spirit – in one sense this is communism in spirit if not in letter.

The photo historian Riccardo Toffoletti helpfully elucidates the difference between Weston's indigenous women and Modotti's: "Where Weston found symmetry Modotti found atmosphere. Modotti's gaze is empathetic." Toffoletti manages to get the difference between their pictures in two short, clear sentences – a remarkable achievement. For Modotti the picturesque and the formal elements were a sideshow, what was fascinating and most important for her were the people and how they managed this social space that they inhabited, these unique places they called home and these curious customs that they called work. Modotti had a keen anthropologist's eye as well as a sensitive artist's and it is this bifocal vision that makes her work so unique and fascinating – hers was a photography of "close observation" – a term used by anthropologists in field work that is well suited here.

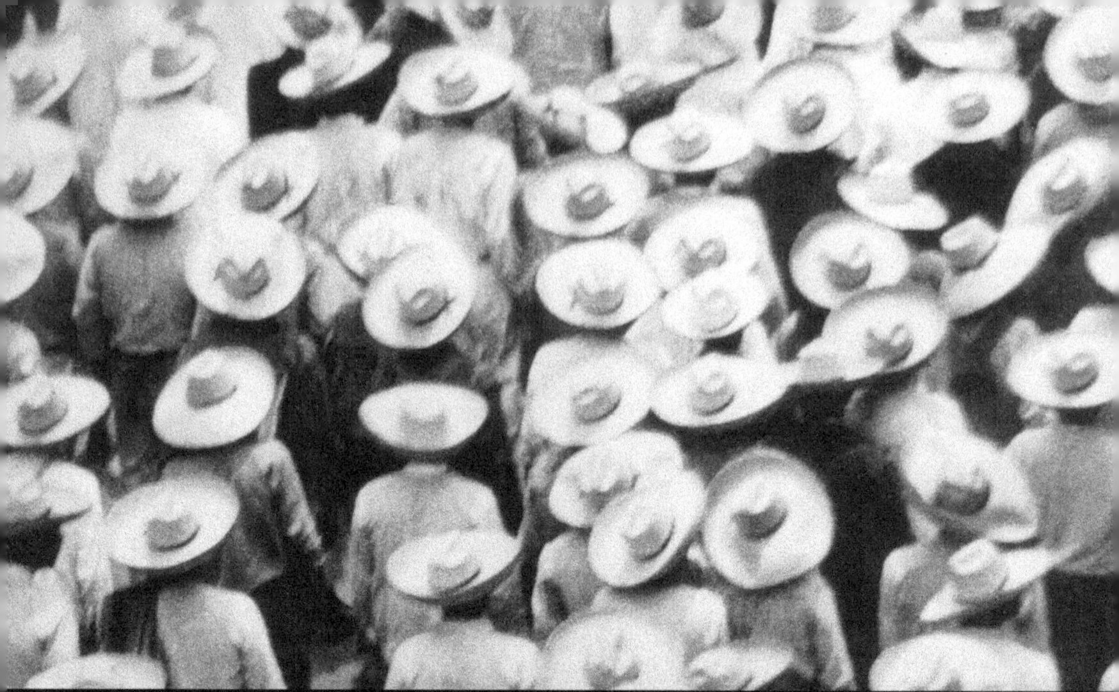

If I could tell my story in words, I wouldn't need to lug around a camera.

Lewis Hine, *Selected Letters*

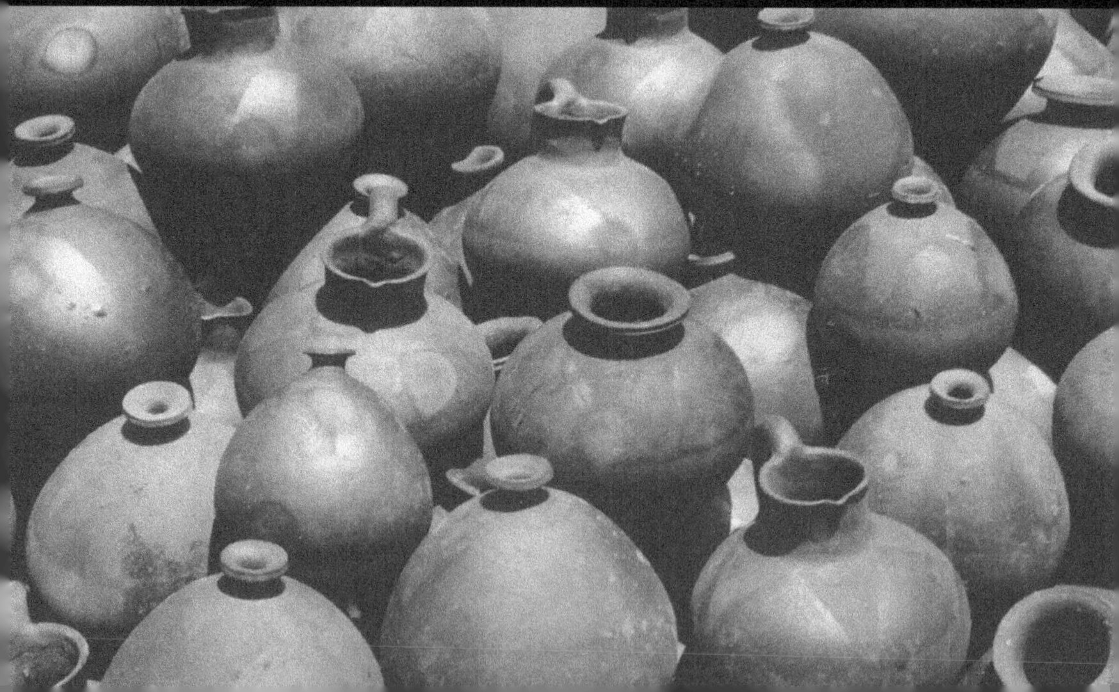

12

The Photography of Concern

Lewis Hine and Jacob Riis

Modotti's *indigenismo* portfolio has some similarities to Lewis Hine and Jacob Riis and it is helpful to see those parallels and differences to understand her thought process. The "photography of concern," that is, a photography devoted to the workers, the underprivileged, the disenfranchised, the dying, etc., begins with Jacob Riis and Lewis Hine. They were both Americans in late 19th and early 20th century New York who referred to their photography as illustrations – they rejected the term "art." Riis, a journalist for the *New York Tribune,* published his first book, *How the Other Half Lives,* in 1890, depicting the slum tenements of New York City and the dark, grimy spaces of the very poor. These were places that many people had heard about but never seen and they became visible for the first time via photography.

Hine, working a decade after Riss, for the National Child Labor Committee, illustrated the need to reform child labor practices, using images with accompanying texts. A 12-hour day for children was considered normal then. Hine followed Riis in attempting to change labor laws by using the inherent realism of photography to affect people emotionally and force them to take political action. In a sense their work was tied thematically to other works of outrage, by writers such as Charles Dickens and Emile Zola, among others, who wrote about child labor in order to upset their readers and, if not move them to take action, at least make them think about the reality that they were inhabiting in a new way.

Jacob Riis wrote that the first glass plates he took, of a mass grave for paupers in New York, was "so dark as to be almost hopeless, but that the very blackness of my picture added a gloom to the show more realistic than any art of professional skill might attain."[77] The pictures had to be as objective and authentic as possible, and they had to function as a window into the world in order to convey the social truths that needed to be fixed. If people thought that the pictures were false or altered in any way – a standard practice from the beginnings of photography familiar to the public – they would likely not be moved to action because they would sense that they were being manipulated. In a sense Riis and Hine had to avoid "art" and any formal considerations that might take away from their desired aim.

Simone de Beauvoir laid out the ethical problem of art, aesthetics, and socially concerned photography succinctly in an essay from 1948 on the ethics of ambiguity:

> Let us say that a writer wants to communicate the horror inspired in him by children working in sweatshops; he produces so beautiful a book that, enchanted by the tale, the style, and even the images, we forget the horror of the sweatshops or even start admiring it. Will we not then be inclined to think that if death, misery, and injustice can be transfigured for our delight, it is not an evil for there to be death, misery and injustice?"[78]

De Beauvoir's text brilliantly lays the problem right at the doorstep of the photography of concern just as the photo magazines and photo agencies were coming into their own, publishing such pictures on a regular basis. Clearly for Riis and Hine the beautiful in such work became a bomb that needed to be defused, making their photographs safe as believable *factual* representations of real life.

Modotti, unlike Riis and Hine, had no problems with art or aesthetics whatsoever but managed to keep it at arm's length long enough to let in the oxygen of "close observation," of documentary, of the thing-itself – it was a balancing act and Modotti became, over time, a master at it. In some cases she went further and played off one to the other in counterpoint – in a manner of speaking the left and the right hand "performed" two distinct "voices" that she held in beautiful tension. In this area she had few equals – perhaps only André Kertész in his early years managed it.

Modotti, possibly because she was Italian, also has no problem with the pleasure or looking. For example, in *Tehuanas in the River* (1929) we see women cleaning clothes and bathing in the river with children. They are all semi-naked or with clothes clinging to their bodies, clearly sexual beings but not sexualized through cliché conventions (see David Hamilton's or Henrik Purienne's pictures of women bathing) because their sexuality coexists with their work, their child caring, their washing before going back to the village – what we see is a *routine* that happens to include sensuous half-naked female bodies. Sensuality and sexuality in Modotti's work is never separate from everyday life. There was no trace of Puritanism in any of her work as there was in Weston's who, despite his many nudes, consistently separated sensuality/sexuality from everyday life – the one exception was his portraits/nudes of Tina Modotti.

Modotti sent some contact prints to Weston from her trip to Oaxaca and Tehuantepec but apologized for the quality, knowing that the snapshot aspect of the series did not fit his aesthetic criteria. What is incredible about her letters to Weston at this time is that she had completely internalized his manner of thinking and, in effect, knew what he was going to think before he did, bringing up explanations and excuses for his presumed objections even before he made them. Nevertheless. Modotti was strong enough to find her own way on this trip to a feminist, matriarchal oasis outside of time, even with apologies to Weston.

Propaganda

As to the question of whether propaganda can be art one would hope that the Soviet experience after 1917 would show that regardless of how vile and destructive a system might be the propaganda to advertise it can, indeed, be art – one need look no further than the work of Gustav Klutsis, Varvara Stepanova or Alexander Rodchenko to promote Soviet style communism.

During the late Twenties Modotti used her camera to make propaganda and her talent had not yet deserted her. She could produce brilliant images such as *Woman With a Flag 1928,* that depicts a young indigenous woman simply dressed in a white skirt carrying a large red flag over her shoulder covering her torso like a shield. Although the image was meant to be on propaganda posters Modotti is unable to control her formalist instincts. She placed the top of the flag square to the top of the frame and the bottom of the flagpole is squared with the balcony in the *azotea* where she set up her shot – not the same *azotea* where she had posed a few years earlier for Weston.

From the same year *Corn, Guitar, Cartridge 1928* is perhaps the greatest revolutionary photograph ever made for propaganda purposes. The image was clearly indebted to Weston's magnificent still life *Sombrero y Huaraches, Mexico, 1926*. But Weston's picture plays with form as it luxuriates on the small details of the beautiful embroidery of the hat and the hand-sewn binding of the soles in the huaraches, while Modotti's image is an open call to Marxist revolution.

The writer Elena Poniatowska suggested that Modotti's work here was influenced by her wide reading, including James Joyce, and the art historian Antonio Saborit took this idea making the connection between Joyce's description – in the first sentence in *Ulysses* where he describes a "bowl of lather on which a mirror and a razor lay crossed" – and the still life with a guitar, cartridge belt and corn cob. That Modotti would have been influenced by her extensive modernist reading makes sense since she was interested not only in literature but also in the new music, particularly Shostakovich, as well as painting, particularly Picasso and the Surrealists, who were also (via André Breton) aligned with the Communist Party. For Poniatowska these are not only images advertising Marxism but emotional portraits of Mexico at that moment that captured not just political enthusiasm but the emergence of a new independent woman, standing on her own.

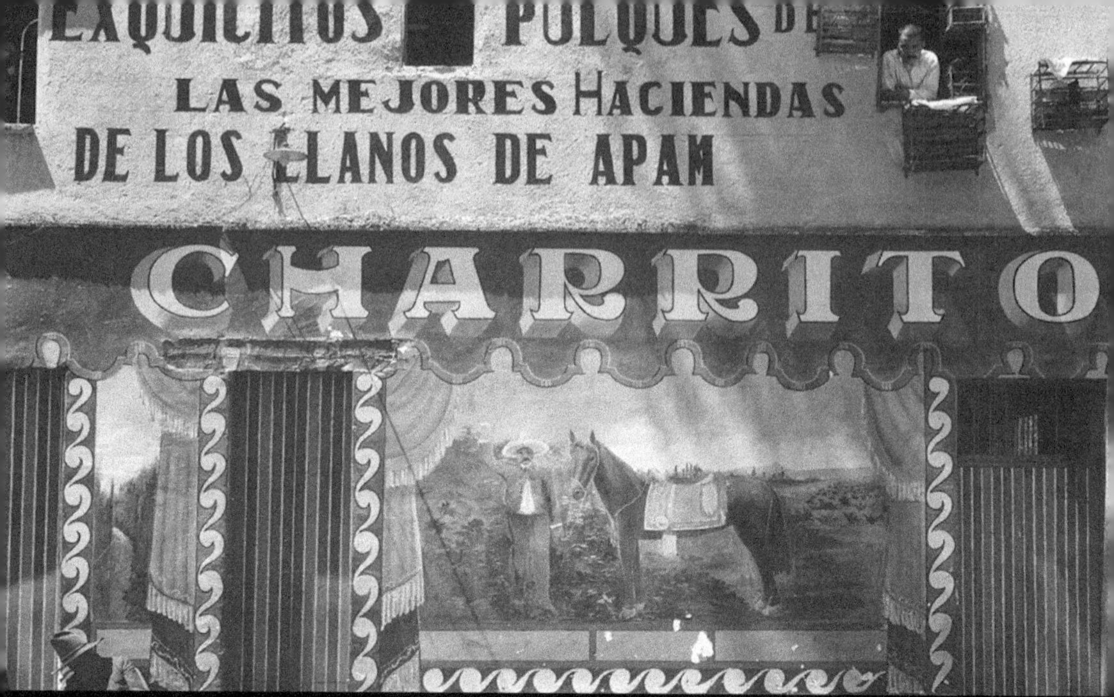

In order to write poetry you must first invent
a poet who will write it.

Antonio Machado

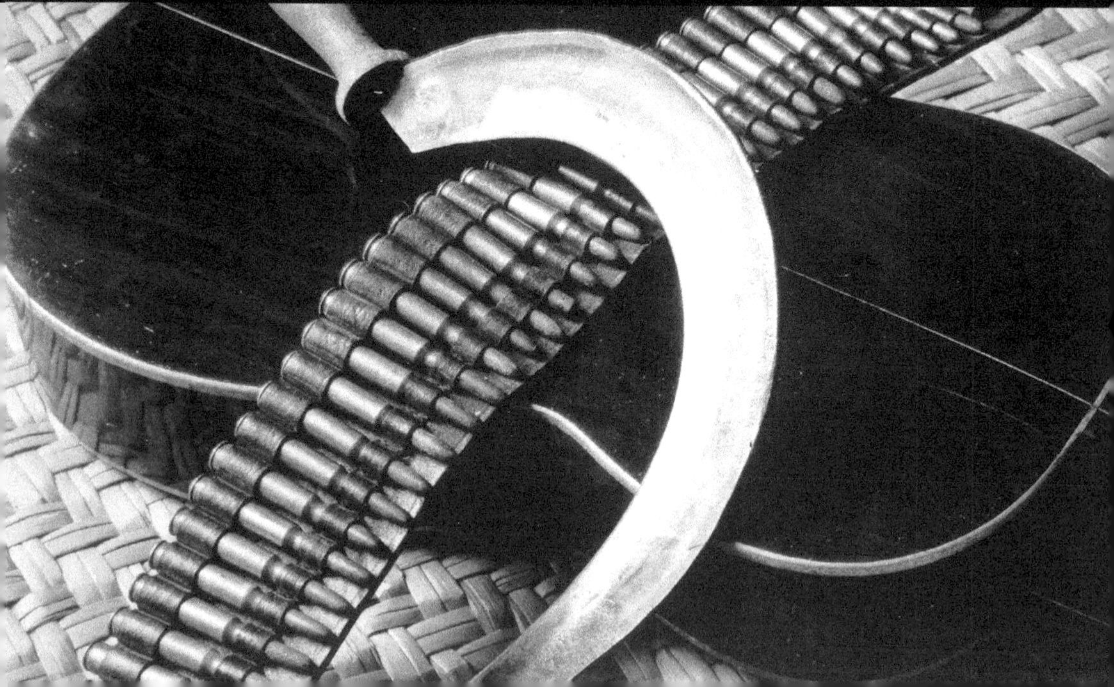

13

The First Revolutionary Exhibition in Mexico!

This Is Your Best Moment

After the trial and acquittal Modotti lay low at the Zamora building and she seemed to be holding it together calmly with a melancholy self-effacement that was typical of her, but Frances Toor, the person who wrote the definitive book on José Posada, who lived in the same building, tells a different story. She recalls that Tina would wake up on some nights screaming in anguish – everyone in the building could hear it.[79] Toor suggested calcium for her nerves but it is not known if she followed this advice – under the circumstances it seems unlikely.

In October of the same year, 1929, the stock market in New York crashed sending shock waves worldwide even to people not directly affected in Mexico and South America. The reason was that the Great Depression that followed was psychological as well as financial. The historian Lucy Moore, who wrote *Anything Goes: A Biography of the Roaring Twenties,* explains:

> The Crash did not cause the Great Depression: that was part of a far broader malaise. What it did was expose the weakness that underpinned the confidence and optimism of the 1920's – poor distribution of income, a weak banking structure and insufficient regulations, the economy's dependence on new consumer goods, the over-extension of industry and the Government's blind belief that promoting business interests would make Americans uniformly prosperous.[80]

Many of the fellow exiles, academics and writers who were the backbone of the Mexican Renaissance were forced to return home. The same thing was happening in Berlin and Paris – an ending to the jazz age beautifully documented by Scott Fitzgerald in *Tender Is the Night* (1934) where one sees that "crack-up" (his term) from the point of view of the wealthy elite on the French Riviera. It is in this environment that Modotti was given the opportunity to show her work in a one-person show – an exhibition that she had been carefully cultivating for years but finally bore fruit on the final days of the decade.

1929 was a busy time for Modotti as a photographer – her reputation as an artist had finally caught up with reality and she was in demand. The letters asking for work were piling up. Antonieta Rivas Mercado, a key figure in cultural promotion in the Twenties in Mexico City who founded an avant-garde theater, Teatro Ulises, was urgently asking her to take pictures of the paintings of Manuel Rodríguez Lozano for collectors. David Alfaro Siqueiros was asking her to participate in a conference he wanted to hold on her work. Orozco needed photos of his murals for a gallery in New York. Magazines like *Forma* also asked Tina to intercede with Weston on their behalf to continue working with them in a new series about the US. Carleton Beals asked for new work on behalf of *Creative Arts* magazine. A group show of photography in Brussels was interested in showing her work, and Willi Münzenberg, another cultural promoter, also wanted prints for a group show in Berlin. Carleton Beals tells her to get on it: "This is your most creative period – this is your best moment."[81]

In the midst of this productive turmoil in December of 1929 Modotti curated and assembled her exhibition at the National Library in Mexico City – part of the National Autonomous University of Mexico, located in the heart of the city. She knew it might be her last chance to put together a coherent body of work from the approximately 400 photographs she had taken over the previous six years. It was a time to take stock. She had gone eyeball-to-eyeball with Edward Weston, one of the great photographers of the century, and managed to equal his work on a variety of occasions in every genre of photography – they were not simply rivals but partners in an adventure of art-making that few people will ever know. Nevertheless, the exhibit was a farewell in a sense to the Mexico she knew and her life there of friends and *tertulias,* parties with Shostakovich playing on the gramophone, or the latest jazz hits, and dressing up as the great "Edward Weston" and doing it so well that even Weston had to laugh and join in the fun. She knew that she was going into the deep end of a political storm from which there would be no going back.

It was not the first time Modotti found her work at the university. In 1926 they had put together a group show with the Fine Arts Club of Mexico in which a few of her pictures were included, but her work had been known since the well-attended exhibit with Weston at the State Museum in Guadalajara in 1925. During the period of 1925–1929 a number of art magazines published her photographs along with reviews of her work keeping her in the public eye, such as *Forma, Horizonte, Creative-Art* and *Mexican Folkways* – the latter was published by Rivera and Frances Toor, while Modotti was officially on the editorial board. This is the context in which Carlos Orozco Romero and Carlos Mérida organized the exhibition. From *Tina Modotti: A New Vision*:

> We know that 1,000 posters, 250 invitations and 5,000 fliers were printed under the photographer's supervision. These numbers indicate how widely the event was disseminated and how extensive the support provided by the University – especially if we consider that in 1929 Mexico City had only approximately 1.7 million inhabitants, and only a small percentage were likely to attend this kind of event.[82]

Unfortunately, full documentation from the exhibit is poor so we have no official list of titles shown. What we have is a photo taken by one of the curators of Modotti wearing all black, hair pulled back in a bun and arms crossed, standing in front of a wall showing her work – she seems to be trying to force a smile but it isn't coming off well. We also have testimony by some critics who wrote reviews and mention some titles. Unfortunately, the prints were numbered so the critics sometimes only refer to numbers. From these sources we can surmise that at least 41 pictures are clearly identified and up to 16 more were probably in the show. Modotti seems to have chosen (as was common at the time) to show her work close together with only a few inches between photos. She printed 11x14-inch or 10x10-inch prints that she showed matted but unframed in a double row hung at eye level. She grouped her prints primarily by genre. One critic mentions an amazing wall of portraits, and from the photo we see the circus tent picture so we know that she showed the early work she had done alongside Weston. From the photograph of her standing in front of her work she clearly made an exception in the organization of work for Mella – his portrait sits atop a double row of pictures by itself, an honorary pride of place – as if Modotti were dedicating the exhibition to him in a photographic sense, without using words. Directly underneath him is a worker carrying a beam and another photo of a hammer and sickle, emblem of the Communist Party – in fact Mella is surrounded by workers and his typewriter, one of the most beautiful still life photographs in her body of work. Modotti herself poses next to *Manos Sosteniendo Una Pala, 1926* (*Hands Holding a Shovel, 1926*) from her series of workers.

On the night of December 3, the exhibition was inaugurated with music and speeches. After the library director introduced the exhibition Concepcioń Michel performed some revolutionary songs. Then the writer José Romano gave an analysis of the work speaking of a "new aesthetic sensibility." There was also a closing event on December 14 where Siqueiros made a speech that historically contextualized Modotti's work and referred to a new direction for photography: "That is one where formalism and social content fused together to create a 'critical vision'...the first revolutionary photographic exhibition in Mexico!"[83] Modotti loved Siquieros's talk and wrote about it to Weston: "I wish you had heard Siqueiros' speech! It was great. Such a profound knowledge of the history of art through the ages and such a vital and significant viewpoint. We were surely smart in getting the program presented. But after the government, the University and all the Mexican politicos pride themselves on their *revolucionarismo,* so they couldn't very well refuse."[84] Modotti refers here to the fact that it had become fashionable for politicians to reference the Revolution and show their independence from Europe and the US, and to unreservedly support "the people" regardless of their political leanings – therefore a "revolutionary photographic exhibition" would be something they would, at least in public, fully support.

The exhibition also allowed Modotti to express herself with a one-page manifesto of photography, starting with a quote by Leon Trotsky: "Technique will become a much more powerful inspiration in artistic production; later, it will find its solution in a higher synthesis of the contrast existing between technique and nature."[85] Biographers all express some shock that Modotti would choose Trotsky, of all people, to quote from since her own Communist friends, especially at Red Aid, would find Trotsky anathema, a "traitor" to the cause. Another problematic aspect of her choice is that many "politicos," as Modotti called them, whether Marxist, liberal or fascist, have little use for art except as decoration or as a teaching tool to "educate the people." Perhaps, as Margaret Hooks suggests, it was a nod to Mella's Trotskyite sympathies.

In any case Trotsky, even in this short quote, seems to be reaching for the stars but having a hard time standing up – a problem he also had in his other writings. Trotsky assumes that art needs a "solution" in a synthesis between technique and nature. How one might create such a synthesis or what it is exactly are, of course, not elaborated upon, probably because no one, including Trotsky, knows what such a synthesis would look like. He seems to be saying that some rapprochement between formalism (technique) and nature (the human animal in the social world) is to be sought for and Modotti, by quoting him, perhaps sees herself as doing that, or trying to do it.

Modotti then begins her short piece titled *"Sobre La Fotografia"* ("About Photography" or "On Photography"): "Whenever the words 'art' or 'artistic' are used with respect to my photographic work I have an unpleasant reaction...I consider myself a photographer and nothing more...Most photographers are still looking for 'artistic effects' or an imitation of other types of graphic expression. These tendencies lead to a hybrid product and do not achieve the most valuable feature that a work should have: PHOTOGRPAHIC QUALITY."[86] (emphasis Modotti) Unlike Trotsky who leaves us hanging Modotti helpfully explains just what constitutes, for her, "photographic quality:" "What should be understood by good photography is that which accepts the limitations inherent in photographic technique, and which takes advantage of all the possibilities and characteristics offered by this medium. Bad photography should be understood as that which is produced, one could say, with a kind of inferiority complex, without valuing what photography has to offer as its very own."[87] This smart use of the term "inferiority complex" is a clear attack on those photographers who wish to make pictures that looked like paintings (abstract or realist), creating "art."

Modotti then gets to the heart of the matter: "Photography, because of the single fact that it can only be produced in the present and based on what objectively exists in front of the camera, is clearly the most satisfactory medium for registering objective life in all its manifestations. For that reason, it has documentary value. If we add to that all of this some sensitivity and understanding of the matter..."[88]

The key word here is "present" – photography gets the present in a way no other art form is able to do. This idea is close to Siegfried Kracauer's "camera reality." For the philosopher Kracauer (writing in 1947) photography engages a realism that should not be confused with realist painting – photography has in its own peculiar DNA – a realism whose ontology questions "a reality within reach." Therefore, the relationship between camera and reality is discrete, tenuous, and ambivalent precisely because of its uncanny mechanical ability to capture the light of a particular moment. The resulting photograph is then a "redemption of physical reality" in which the realist and formal aspects can only be understood together as a whole. Moreover, because there is a consciousness behind the camera, for Kracauer the photograph records but may also reveal, that is, we may perceive not only a specific mediated reality but what lies underneath it.

This philosophical approach to the medium fits well into Modotti's ideas that she presented to her audience in the first, and last, one-person exhibition of her work in her lifetime. It is also the only time that we hear her "voice" speaking for herself about photography.

It is clear from her short essay that she has spent years thinking about photography, has seen various schools and read various theories, and has come to her own conclusions that are delivered without any academic affections or coy references – she is blunt and to the point, articulate without being verbose, intelligent without being pedantic – she clearly understands her own work and its relation to photographic history at that moment – it's an admirable text but unfortunately the last word we have from her on photography – she never wrote about the medium again.

That same year there was an assassination attempt on the President of Mexico, Pascual Ortiz Rubio – the crackdown was severe and swift. Rubio's cry of "return to order" enters the Mexican Renaissance like someone switching the lights on during an all-night party. The offices of *El Machete* were ransacked and shut down – many gathering places were raided and arrests made. There was a large, well-organized anti-immigrant, anti-Communist campaign that also went after "bloody Tina Modotti." Mexico broke relations with the USSR and asked their consulate to return to Moscow. Many Communists and even sympathizers who were not officially members of the Party were permanently exiled from Mexico – some went back home, others without families went to Europe to continue "the good fight." Between the Crash of 1929, the Great Depression that followed, and Rubio's crackdown on anything smacking of "avant-garde" or "socialist" the Mexican Renaissance came to an end – it had lasted exactly the decade of the Twenties.

Modotti was imprisoned and isolated for two weeks where conditions were, as one would expect in a Mexican prison at that time, horrifying. It was possible that she might be tried again in one of the many "plots" being uncovered daily. Tina was rightfully terrified of another round with the police and the press as it is unlikely she would have survived it. Finally, Modotti was released and given 48 hours to leave the country. She gave away her books and sold her photographic equipment to Manuel Álvarez Bravo. Much has been made of Modotti selling her equipment as proof that she gave up photography but, given the time frame and her finances, she had little choice.

Modotti decided to move to Berlin, where she spoke the language (from living in Austria as a child) and didn't need a visa (being Italian). She also had a few connections there including Willi Münzenberg who was well connected with the art world and had mastered the ability to shift socially from leftist political meetings with bad coffee and cigarettes to capitalist deals with wealthy aristocrats, over fine champagne, with ease. He had a rare gift for making friends from all sides of the political spectrum – an invaluable talent in times of trouble. Berlin was a city then in the grips of a political maelstrom as the Weimar Republic was in its final death throes before succumbing to Nazism in 1933 – everything was unraveling and there was no way to stop it. Modotti was also an enormous fan of the work of George Grosz and Käthe Kollwitz, both still living then in Berlin, and hoped to meet them – her friend Münzenberg said he could arrange it but unfortunately the meeting never took place. She wasn't in Berlin long enough to establish herself, make any new contacts, or develop any friends.

14

Tina Modotti's War

Undercover With Vittorio Vidali

In the new decade, starting at the beginning of 1930 Modotti started a relationship – her last – with Vittorio Vidali, an Italian-born exile who was working for Red Aid and whom she met while working on the Sacco and Vanzetti demonstrations. This was a cover for his more clandestine work as he had been trained in Moscow and sent to Mexico City to help propaganda efforts as well as to supervise a clandestine network of surveillance, espionage and small-scale covert operations including the violent targeting of prominent anti-Stalinists – this involved plotting assassinations and subverting the political work of adversaries of all stripes, whether from the left or the right. As to be expected Vidali had no feeling for art, music or photography – like Mella he was a committed revolutionary who prided himself on his focus and getting the job done.

Despite Modotti's hardline political stand her communication with Weston reveals that she had in fact not lost her deep affection for formalist photography, the sublime, art, etc. On the contrary – perhaps because she felt the need to suppress it publicly her feelings intensified. Early in 1930 Weston sent Tina some images of the work entitled *Pepper* (1930). This was her response:

> "Edward, nothing has affected me more than these photographs; I simply can't look at them for a long time without feeling perturbed – they are disquieting not just mentally but physically. There is something so pure here but also so perverse, containing all the innocence of natural objects as well as the morbidity of a refined and even distorted mind. They make me think of lilies and embryos at the same time – they are mystical and erotic."[89]

One doubts she put this much emotion and this much thought into her letters to her friends at Red Aid or the Communist Party.

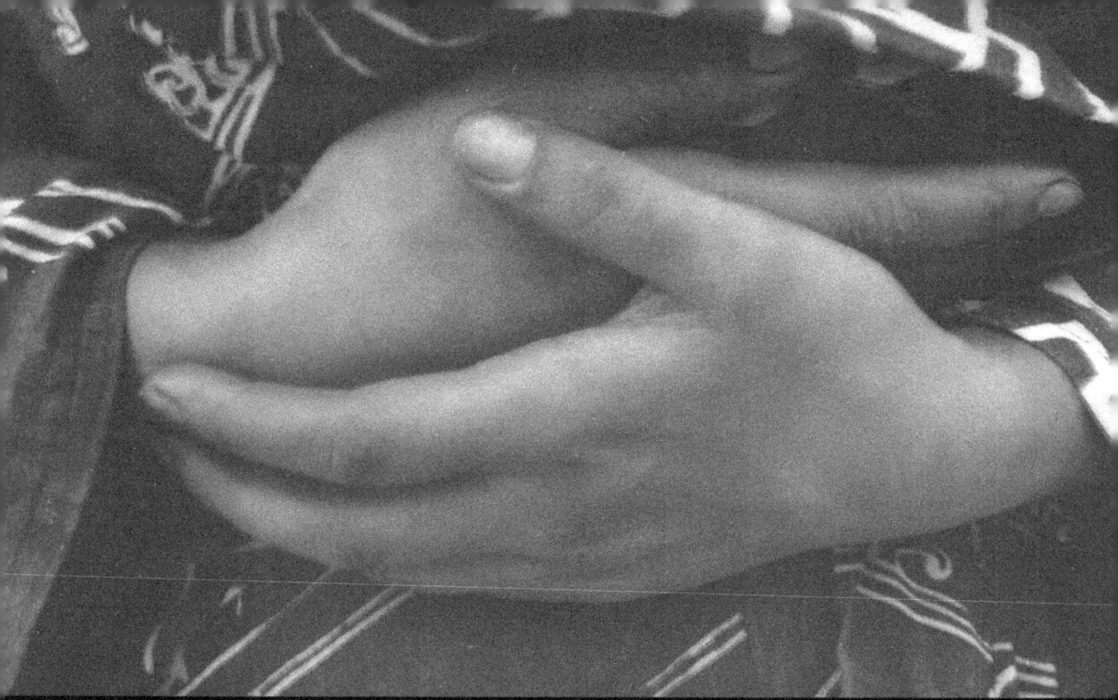

I had it bad. The empty camera trembled in my hand.

Robert Capa, *Slightly Out of Focus: An Autobiography*

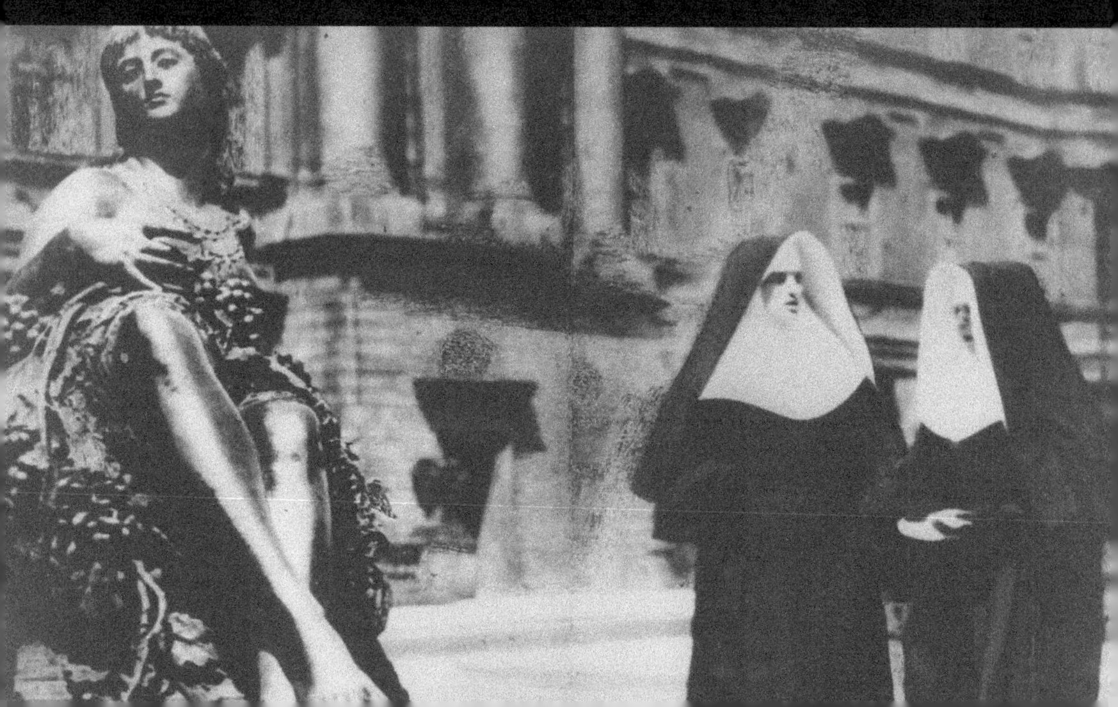

Vidali incredibly managed to find himself on the same boat as Modotti headed to Rotterdam, the port of destination, and it is here that they tentatively became a couple. Vidali knew not only how to find, and then fit into people's schedules, but also how to make himself emotionally indispensable. Despite trying to put a good face on the situation her letters to Weston, again, show a different side of her: unsure and distraught, physically and emotionally exhausted, devastated that just as her career as a photographer was taking off she had to leave, maybe forever. She confessed to Weston in a long letter that outlined her grievances that she had almost gone crazy but was persevering by keeping her focus on her political work. While Modotti returned eventually to Mexico years later she never saw her friends again, but in a sense, she had already said goodbye.

Berlin

In Berlin friends and comrades went out of their way to help, including the photographer Johanna Alexandra, known as Lotte Jacobi, a high-energy American exile who was well connected in Berlin. She offered Modotti the use of her studio and the possibility of a regular income from Jacobi's own successful photo-agency that hired photographers for shoots that were rudimentary but paid a decent income.

Jacobi was a go-getter who didn't wait for men to give her work or agencies to send her on assignment. She started her own agency and sold her work commercially to clients dealing with everything from advertising, portraits, magazine work, and photojournalism but her personal work was a series of informal, high-contrast portraits of figures from avant-garde artistic, theatrical, and intellectual circles from the Weimar Republic in natural, seemingly spontaneous, poses that delved into psychological nuances. Influenced by expressionist cinema and the work of Félix Nadar she photographed people in their own environments, talking to them while she worked to put them at ease. Her work was brilliant as we can see in her iconic photograph of Berlin chanteuse Lotte Lenya (1928) and her dapper, metalinguistic self-portrait (1937).

She encouraged Modotti to abandon her bulky equipment and move to a smaller camera that she was willing to loan out. The new Leica 35mm was all the rage then because of its flexibility and compactness. The camera could easily fit in a purse – or a hat, as Erich Salomon did to surreptitiously photograph members of the Berlin government as they, in a lull between wars, debated a new world order. When the Pact of Paris was signed in 1928 by heads of state that had participated in WWI, presumably ensuring that such a tragic and useless war would never happen again, Salomon was there with his hidden camera sometimes concealed in his briefcase or his hat. Salomon looked like he belonged – always smoking a cigar and insisting on being called "Herr Doctor" by anyone who approached him. By this surreptitious use of a hidden camera Salomon jump-started a more aggressive form of photojournalism, or paparazzi photography, still in effect today. Salomon was the first photojournalist before the term even existed but unfortunately his tenure as a master photographer was short-lived due to the war that came, despite the fine treaty – Salomon, a German Jew, died in Auschwitz in 1944.

Modotti refused the kind offer from Jacobi and she later shared her thoughts with Weston in a letter: "I know the material found on the streets is rich and wonderful, but my experience is that the way I am accustomed to work, slowly planning my composition etc. is not suited for such work. By the time I have the composition or expression right the picture is gone. I guess I want to do the impossible and therefore I do nothing."[90]

Something interesting about her letters to Weston at this time is that they constantly refer to photography, to her favorite poet, the romantic modernist Antonio Machado, and to their friends in Mexico City but never to politics or her work for Red Aid – that softer side of her was allowed to come forward in her letters but she is at this point, quite literally, heading into the trenches of a war in Europe where there will be no place for poems or pictures of calla lilies. Here is a poem by Machado that might apply here:

> I would like to see you and not see you
> I would like to talk with you and not talk
> I would like to find you alone
> And I wouldn't want to find you.
> Sorrow and sorrow that is not
> Yesterday I was aching to see you
> Today I grieve
> Because I saw you
> And I think it's heartbreaking.

The Workers Pictorial Newspaper

Despite what she told Weston she did try street photography but with her trusty large format Graflex – her favorite camera. Modotti would choose a promising site, set up her camera and then wait for people – again the human element – to step into the shot and hopefully do something interesting. The resulting shots taken in Berlin have a strangely facile, ironic quality. The photograph of an overweight couple at the zoo, looking like strange animals that might be exhibits themselves, is certainly amusing and another photograph of two nuns passing a neoclassical statue depicting a vigorous young naked woman is whimsical. Elliot Erwitt can do this kind of shot and he brings the energy and enthusiasm of fresh discovery to it (whatever the merits of the shot might be) but clearly here Modotti herself is uninterested. She seems to have had no feeling for unplanned, chance encounters that are brief and evanescent – the essence of street photography. Despite Berlin's fascinating visual cacophony Modotti seemed strangely uninvolved. There was no energy, ideas or curiosity present. The life had gone out of the work. She eventually described these pictures to Weston in another letter as "crap."[91]

Still, the Berlin trip was not completely a loss. Jabobi got magazines to show her old work and pay her for it, including the hugely popular *AIZ* (*Arbeiter-Illustirerte-Zeitung*), (*The Workers Pictorial Newspaper*). Despite the paper's hard pro-Communist stand it had wide distribution not only in Germany but all over Europe and beyond. The reason was the magazine, unlike most humorless Communist journals, had a very sarcastic, ribald and ironic sense of humor that was primarily visual and didn't need subtitles. Its most prominent contributors were the photomontage master John Heartfield and the artist George Grosz. Jacobi also managed to convince Modotti to do a one-person show in her apartment so friends and admirers could come see for themselves the work of her brilliant new friend. She used Jacobi's darkroom to make her own prints but unfortunately no documentation or photographs exists of this informal showing of her work.

She was also encouraged to photograph workers at a factory – a promising subject that would be of interest to her as it would seem a great place to photographically play off workers and industrial machinery in the modern era. Nevertheless, when Modotti found out that the workers had their own photo club where they would exhibit pictures of each other she balked, saying in letters that she felt taken aback by going to a place where the workers were already photographing themselves "probably much better" than she ever could as an outsider. It was a lost opportunity as Modotti seems to suffer, still, from a certain self-deprecation, a certain uncertainty, unaware that she could bring to the table an anthropological and artistic sensitivity that the workers – for all of their inside knowledge – might not have and might, in fact, appreciate.

Berlin had become a city with travelers coming in to see the collapse of a vibrant and exciting civilization firsthand and take advantage of the German currency that was almost valueless – as to be expected sexual predators invaded the city as did wealthy businessmen buying up buildings and art for a steal – Berlin was in the midst of a fire sale. While you had poverty tourism on the one hand on the other you had thousands trying to flee the city before the Nazis took over and started their well-outlined program for a "thousand-year Reich." In the midst of this chaos there was a photographic boom happening not only in Berlin but all through Germany as we can see from the aforementioned workers photo-club and the famous *Film und Foto* exhibition held in Stuttgart in 1929 featuring the most innovative and important photographs produced in the Weimar period primarily from Germany but also from Russia and France.

The exhibition included work by Jacobi herself as well as Alexander Rodchenko, Pierre Boucher, Man Ray, François Kollar and another woman photographer, Florence Henri. Unlike Modotti Henri was lucky in that she started early apprenticing with Fernand Léger and later at the Bauhaus she studied with László Moholy-Nagy – you could not ask for a better start. She dove into the deep end of the avant-garde becoming, at a young age, one of the most prominent photographers in Europe. Unfortunately, she and Modotti never met as when Tina was in Berlin Florence was in Paris, where she established a studio and taught classes – her most famous pupil was Lisette Model. Paris then was at the center of another photographic revolution similar to the one taking place in literature with Joyce and Eliot. Aside from Henri, Brassaï, Germaine Krull, Cartier-Bresson, Claude Cahun and various expatriates such as Man Ray and André Kertész were all in Paris, opening an important new chapter for the medium. Despite this passionate milieu Henri grew dissatisfied, eventually giving up photography to become an abstract painter.

While Modotti arrived too late for the New Vision exhibit she would surely have heard about it from Jacobi who was there and showed her work alongside Man Ray, whose work she loved, and other master photographers. Tina's work surely belonged there as well and she must have sensed it – it had to hurt – as there are only so many chances like that in a lifetime to show your work and get that kind of exposure. While her timing for the Mexican Renaissance had been spot-on in Europe everything seemed off kilter – the timing was off, and sadly, it was never set right again.

Modotti's fusion of formalist photography with documentary has much in common with the New Vision movement particularly the work of László

Moholy-Nagy, its founder (who came up with the name "New Vision"), who was more open and defiant of photographic conventions, using radical cropping and surrealist juxtapositions that would have been close to Modotti's own thinking. Despite Moholy-Nagy's formalist credentials, he, like Modotti, also used the conventions of the "snapshot" but put quotes around it treating it as part of the vocabulary of photography that could be used in counterpoint to other formal characteristics within the photograph. They both held a beautiful balance between photography's "poetics" (now in quotes) and its "documentary" (ditto) aspect in perfect balance or tension.

Unlike Modotti, always on the run, living out of a suitcase, always looking over her shoulder, Moholy-Nagy was a highly regarded teacher at the prestigious Bauhaus school. He had his own apartment on site where he lived with his wife Lucia who was also a photographer. Lucia is remembered now for her iconic shot from 1925 of her husband, off-center, raising his hand toward the camera lens, smiling with easy bonhomie. It perfectly combines avant-garde aesthetics with the snapshot, a film still that encapsulates a whole film with a supremely light touch – something very difficult to do.

Moholy-Nagy and had all the time in the world to take photographs and even write a book-length manifesto titled *Painting, Photography, Film* originally published in Germany in 1925. Interestingly in this book Moholy-Nagy used the work of Alfred Stieglitz as an example of "incorrect photography," that is, work that is influenced by painterly effects. Moholy-Nagy was not officially a member of the Party but was a leftist sharing with the Constructivists and the German Communist Party (and Modotti) the idea that art, technology and industry together could be used to reorder society toward an egalitarian Eden where the "blind dynamics of competition and profit" (Rosa Luxemburg) would be phased away creating a new socially coherent and rational society. Moholy-Nagy eventually became something of an *éminence grise* but in the Twenties he was approachable and loved photographers – it's a shame he never encountered Modotti as their interaction would undoubtedly have been fascinating.

The honeymooning Anita Brenner also visited Europe in 1930 and stopped in Berlin, from Paris, to enjoy the Weimar Republic in its final moments. Knowing that Tina was in town she went to see her old friend. What she saw scared her. She wrote in her journal that she got "the willies" from the way Modotti clung to Stalinist jargon and for the way she parroted Party slogans robotically.[92] Clearly from the sudden decline of her work, the desperate letters to Weston. and Brenner's assessment, we can say that Modotti was in trouble. Her only direction in life seemed to come from the Comintern, an organization based in Moscow to promote worldwide revolution that she had been introduced to by Vidali. Modotti wrote regularly to Weston that she was thinking of giving up photography but was uncertain about what else she was equipped to do.

In their superb catalog for the exhibition at the Whitechapel Gallery in London titled *Frida Kahlo and Tina Modotti* Laura Mulvey and Peter Wollen put forth the idea that Tina gave up photography because she could not show in galleries or museums only in magazines and newspapers, becoming in effect a journalist, something she never aspired to do. This is how they put it:

> Faced with the problem to "journalize" her art Modotti gave it up altogether. She belonged, in a sense, to a previous epoch, in which photography was an artisanal product, closer despite the modernity of its technology, to folk art or popular urban art than to the mass media...While in Germany her photographs were taken up and published in illustrated magazines, in Mexico City they were shown in exhibitions, mounted and hanging on a wall like paintings. This was not simply a question of art in opposition to journalism, but of quite different ways of contextualizing and looking at photographs.[93]

Mulvey and Wollen's argument seems well thought out here and reasonable but I am not in agreement with it. Neither Weston nor Modotti seem to have had a problem with the "journalizing" of their photo work and both enjoyed working with various magazines in Mexico. Even after Weston returned to California he worked regularly with photo journals such as *Life* as a viable way to make money and get his work known to a wider public who would ordinarily never set foot in a gallery or museum.

More egregiously (from my perspective) the reference to Modotti's discomfort with "mass media" refers to Walter Benjamin's famous essay "Art in the Age of Mechanical Reproduction" in which he posits that the more avant-garde or advanced artists would not only recognize and accept the new "mechanical reproduction" techniques but openly use them to full advantage to make a new sort of art. From this perspective Modotti would be an "artisanal" artist because she favored galleries over magazines but Rodchenko would be an "advanced" artist since he favored magazines – even advertising – over the gallery.

But is Walter Benjamin right? To understand Wollen/Mulvey's use of Benjamin's ideas let's use as an example the work of Andy Warhol, who would be seen as an "advanced" artist because he used mass-reproduction techniques (the silkscreen, photography, cinema), while Philip Guston, a contemporary of Warhol's, who painted on canvas using European oil paints (and sometimes even an easel!), would be seen as a retrograde "artisanal" artist insisting on maintaining "traditional" models of Western art that were anachronistic. But is Warhol in fact a better or more "advanced" artist than Guston? Whatever one's tastes may be the question remains an open one surely and not an open-and-shut case, as Benjamin's essay would suggest.

The other problem with Mulvey and Wollen's conclusion is that it is not at all clear that Modotti gave up photography. She certainly did not pursue it as she had in Mexico but there are examples of her work from Berlin, and one from Moscow, and there are also accounts of her carrying a camera in Spain but no pictures survive that would prove it. Her work in Berlin *Mother and Child, 1930* shows a pregnant woman with two children. It's a rudimentary shot (for her) but has her characteristic off-center framing that we know from her work in Mexico. Most conclusively of all Modotti, in a letter to Weston from Germany, states that she is thinking of giving up photography, but that fact alone shows that she has not given up photography.

What is certain is that there was a retreat from photography as a full-time occupation and that it was precipitated by two events, her move to Europe, where she was living out of a suitcase, and her new relationship with Vidali; this was a man who had no interest in photography and would have found someone like Weston to be merely a vulgar bourgeois aesthete who makes pretty pictures for rich people to decorate their homes, paid for by the exploitation of the working classes. Modotti would have had a hard time explaining to such a man why she was making artful pictures that were politicized without being journalized. For Vidali these considerations would seem like splitting hairs – of what importance was "art" when the world was burning?

What is more likely is that Modotti suppressed her photographic work in favor of political activism as her new man was an exemplar of "political activist" par excellence. But as her own reading of Freud, that she did in her days in Los Angeles, would have explained the more you repress something as important as the artistic impulse the more you force that repression to manifest itself as neurosis and self-destructive behavior. Her own depression that deepened as she went on this strange ersatz sabbatical through Europe and Russia might be seen as a trial by fire – a punishment of sorts that she felt must be endured for a higher cause, or perhaps it was simply a form of atonement.

In her letters to Weston she also writes that she was completely unprepared for the life of Berlin: "The strain shows on the people; they never laugh, they walk the streets very gravely, always in a hurry and seem to be constantly conscious of the heavy burden which weighs on their shoulders."[94] Tina was also ill-prepared for the climate, with freezing temperatures and no sunshine in her first two weeks in the city. She also noted that in Berlin there was a photo studio on almost every corner all displaying good work while in Mexico she had felt special.

Another problem for her was that she was used to earning her own income and being independent as she had been working for a living since she was 11 years old. After Weston left for California she had relied on her healthy portrait business and photographing artworks, but now she was reliant on handouts from Red Aid and Vidali to pay expenses – her self-assurance was coming undone. Homesick for Mexico and bitter about having to start over at the worst possible moment for her career she complained to Weston that "for one coming from Mexico the change is rather cruel. But I know that the wisest thing is just to forget the sun, the blue skies and other delights of Mexico and adapt myself to this new reality and start, once more, life all over again."[95] One senses here despair and resignation – clearly Modotti was at her wit's end.

From Berlin Tina considered a return to Italy, as part of her family in San Francisco – running from the periodic anti-immigrant, Red witch hunts in the US – had relocated to Trieste, a city that Modotti and the family knew from previous experience as Udine was very close to Trieste, then a beautiful port town that was, despite its small size, multilingual and cosmopolitan. Vidali finally convinced her that Italy was off-limits due to Mussolini's fascist police, and they should move to the Soviet Union where he had connections that could provide them with work and a place to live. The British writer Christopher Isherwood was in Berlin at the same time as Modotti and Vidali (1929–1933) to witness it all – though there is no record that they ever met – and he managed to write a great short novel called *Goodbye to Berlin* that got the manic energy, the decadence on a budget, the terrifying and wonderful new liberating freedoms, the lightning in a bottle about to explode aspect of the Berlin that Modotti would have known but, unfortunately, could not represent in her art.

USSR

After only a few months in Germany, in October 1930 Modotti pared down her possessions yet again, said goodbye to her Berlin friends and with Vidali took the train to the USSR. Moscow in 1930 was another city in the throes of catastrophic changes, rampant poverty and a massive housing shortage. Vidali only managed to get an apartment through his secret police connections. In Moscow, as in Berlin, there was a confusing influx and effluence of refugees seeking shelter from the storm as some were coming in from countries torn apart by the depression and others were fleeing the pogroms, famine and gulags of Stalin's "new society."

Once in Moscow Modotti discovered that Vidali had been in the service of the Soviet secret police the GPU, the predecessor of the KGB, for years. There was also another woman, a Russian who was pregnant with Vidali's child, but as to be expected Vidali had no interest in starting a family with anyone – the Party was his family. Patricia Albers tries to put this malevolent aspect of the "the good fight" – an often-used communist expression of their struggle – in some perspective: "Tina was a woman very passionate about the idea [of Communism] mused one comrade; it was reflected in her gaze, in her voice, and almost anything done in the name of the idea, the victory of the proletariat, seemed justifiable. Whether robbing banks or dispensing with enemies of the people, 'revolutionary necessity' had long been part and parcel of Bolshevik culture."[96]

Modotti seemed to be either unaware or indifferent to what the historian Martin Malia referred to as the "extraordinary dynamism and horror that characterized the Soviet experiment."[97] This "experiment" included the torture and execution of millions (from 1917 to 1953), including children who died by the thousands in the terror-famines instigated by Lenin in a haphazard way and then more systematically administered by Stalin. That it would be necessary to torture and kill untold millions to create a credible alternative to capitalism seems so naïve that it is difficult to imagine anyone of Modotti's intelligence and sensitivity succumbing to this fantasy. But the evidence overwhelmingly supports that she was not alone within the intellectual class in subscribing to Stalinist ideology or in helping to expand its reach. As Martin Amis succinctly put it: "He [Stalin] tortured, not to force you to reveal a fact, but for you to collude in a fiction."[98]

When Vidali spoke of a "job" Modotti perhaps thought it might be related to photo-lab work or translation but what he had in mind was that she was recruited as a Soviet agent to carry money, names of informants, and orders to agents abroad, traveling to Hungary, Romania and other hot spots using her Red Aid credentials as cover. This was highly sensitive, dangerous work – if caught she would undoubtedly have been tortured to get information from her, but once the offer was on the table Modotti accepted the job without saying a word about it.

Although she was in the Soviet Union at the height of Constructivism and the revolution in art, graphic design and photography that was taking place in Moscow there is no record of her involvement with any of it, either as a spectator or a participant. She makes no mention of Rodchenko or the other radical photographic work being done at that time in Moscow by Boris Ignatovich, Alexander Ustinov and others. Whether she was aware of their work or not is hard to say but seems likely since it must have at least come up in conversations she had with locals in the Moscow scene.

She did meet with Sergei Eisenstein, who had just returned to Moscow from Mexico where his film *Que Viva México!* (1930) had been terminated during production by Upton Sinclair who was financing the maestro's film about the Mexican Revolution. Interestingly Eisenstein had taken a page or two from Brenner's work by creating a palimpsest of sorts between the Aztec's series of armed revolts against the Spanish and the later uprisings in 1910 fashioning his own version of syncretism. He was familiar with Weston/Modotti's work as he had used images from Brenner's *Idols Behind Altars* as inspiration to storyboard his work – an aspect of preproduction in which Eisenstein was meticulous – and he acknowledged the book as an influence on the film.[99]

Eisenstein had also seen Modotti's portfolio because Jay Leyda, the American film historian and specialist in Soviet cinema, carried it with him in Moscow for a New York gallery dealer named Alma Reed, hoping to sell some of the pictures. When Eisenstein was asked in an interview who the best photographers in the world were, he replied, "Tina Modotti is the best." [100] Unfortunately, Modotti, as far as we know, never photographed the photogenic Eisenstein – it would have been fascinating to see what Tina would have made of him. Photographers invariably sought out Eisenstein knowing he was a great subject. Among the best of these portraits is Germaine Krull's own version of Weston's "heroic heads" – her portrait of Eisenstein from 1930 when he was briefly in Paris – where she plays with focus and movement within a tight frame, demonstrating the brief but fruitful collaboration, or cross-pollination, of ideas between photographers, painters and avant-garde filmmakers in the early 20th century – a renaissance that would not be seen again until the 1960s where it had its final flowering, all sparks, loud colors, new sounds, and sharp angles.

The one photograph of Modotti from her Moscow years that has survived is titled *Young Pioneers in the Soviet Union* (1932) which is credited to her but could easily be by any one of the photographers working in Moscow at that time. The picture shows four boys, two of them carrying the Communist red flag. The old artful wall behind them has a dark band at the top that is square with the picture plane – the only perfunctory nod to formalist aesthetics. The picture is so by-the-book propaganda that many similar pictures of Nazi youth from the same period can be found, including by Modotti's younger (by six years) contemporary Leni Riefenstahl, who would soon start working for the Nazis making propaganda films and photography.

Modotti was also visited in Moscow by Lotte Jacobi. Because Jacobi was Jewish and close to leftist and communist circles she was forced to flee Berlin returning home to New York, but before heading west she took a trip east to Moscow to see the famous "society of the future" for herself. Jacobi offered to help Modotti find her footing in New York where she had many connections but Tina explained that the authorities would not permit her entry into the country – she was on a list of radical undesirables. In any case Vidali and Modotti were being sent by Red Aid to a new destination where they were needed: Spain.

Spain

Modotti and Vidali arrived in Spain in 1936, sent by the Comintern on clandestine work to Madrid. Unlike Berlin or Moscow where her stay was limited to a few months Vidali and Modotti were in Spain for three years (1936–1939). Tina again arrived in a country being ripped apart by economic disintegration, political polarization and social unrest – to add to that list Spain was also in the midst of a civil war. In short order she seemed to be taking a grand tour of the highlights of 20th-century cities at their most disastrous and dramatic historical moment. To add to the undercover element further Vidali was known as "Commandante Carlos" and Modotti used the pseudonym "Maria Ruiz." Modotti seems to have stepped into a mirror world from her Hollywood days but now the bad melodramas that she used to laugh at were real.

Interestingly the great photographers Endre Friedmann and Gerta Pohorylle were also in Spain at the same time as Modotti. Endre and Gerta were a couple, like Edward and Tina, but eventually changed their names to Robert Capa and Gerda Taro (Capa via Frank Capra the Hollywood director and Taro via Greta Garbo, the Hollywood star). The Hungarian Capa and the German Taro changed – or Americanized – their names to make it easier to get their photographs published in presses and distributed by photo agencies. The ploy worked and they both became, like Modotti, celebrity photographers, but unlike Modotti they showed their work exclusively through newspapers and magazines – only later after they were both killed in action (Taro in Spain and Capa in Vietnam) did they enter the ivory halls of the gallery/museum world. Both of them sold work to agencies under the name "Robert Capa" that guaranteed a better income. Arguably, they were then the best working photographers in the world using the new smaller 35mm cameras. They thought of themselves as "bearing witness" and "opening the eyes of the world" to the fight against fascism so clearly they were not, in any sense, neutral. Capa even had the temerity to advise his elder colleague (by 5 years) Henri Cartier-Bresson to drop the "artist" label and call himself a "photojournalist" because "then you can do anything."

Neither the dapper, intellectual Cartier-Bresson nor Modotti/Weston ever took up that challenge. The 35mm format that Modotti had rejected (after the offer in Berlin) was the tool of choice for Capa/Taro. Unlike larger formats the camera was an extension of the body – with that format you are part (or can become a part) of the current and flow of an event because you are *inside* the experience; it becomes a way of taking in fast-moving action and capturing it with ease. After all, 35mm film was used before the invention of the Leica with movie film in Europe and Hollywood – it is a format made for movement. With larger formats you are always outside, always the "objective" observer. When one sees videos of Cartier-Bresson shooting it looks like he's dancing, because he is trying to find the flow, with his camera always an extension of his dance - the Leica was the perfect tool for him to make "art." We remember that Modotti didn't like dancing – perhaps this can account, at least in part, for her inability to resonate with the possibilities of the 35mm format. For Taro it was the opposite. Her work in larger formats is somewhat stilted and formal but with the 35mm camera she found her voice – in Spain she even became known as "the girl with the Leica." In any case, it would have been unlikely the daring, romantic team of Capa/Taro would have met Modotti as she was primarily in Madrid and Barcelona doing clandestine work and they were mostly on the front lines where Taro was eventually mortally injured while riding on a running board in a car that collided with a tank.

Modotti and Vidali landed in Spain shortly after the civil war started in July 1936 as the left/socialist Popular Front (or Republicans) stepped into power landing an early victory that would soon fade as Franco and the fascists, with the help of Hitler and Mussolini, quickly recovered ground. With the allies not willing to help the Spanish Second Republic – because many of their members were openly Communists – the days of the Republic were numbered. Hitler saw an opening that could provide a vital new front alongside Italy. While in Spain Modotti received news that her mother had died – they hadn't seen each other in 10 years. She didn't mention it and stuck to the job at hand that she performed with total dedication, never noting it in her letters that began to dwindle – clearly Tina was withdrawing.

In her clandestine work Modotti at times dressed as a nun working in hospitals as a nurse, gathering information. Her predecessor – an actual nurse – was a Fascist sympathizer who had poisoned several Republicans and Popular Front veterans. After her execution by firing squad Red Aid decided to put one of their own on the job. As part of Modotti's clandestine work she had to act as an informant. Inevitably such a job, sooner or later, lands one on shaky moral ground. For Modotti it happened in 1938 when she denounced a 25- year-old Brazilian career soldier Alberto Besouchet. He was accused of having had relations with an "adventuress," a Brazilian singer associated with an underground Trotsky group. He was asked by the Comintern to write a letter denouncing Trotsky as a traitor but Besouchet refused. While this was a commendable act morally it sealed his fate. He was executed by firing squad at the end of 1938 during the Popular Front's final retreat from Barcelona.

The charge against Besouchet of consorting with an "adventuress" is strange since Modotti herself – in one of her earlier incarnations – could easily have fit that description. Modotti's old friends in Mexico, Diego Rivera and Frida Kahlo, were public supporters of Trotsky – would Modotti inform on them if the same situation arose? Fortunately for her the question never arose, but perhaps she thought about it when she was away from the Comintern's watchful eyes. No doubt Rivera and Kahlo thought about it too and stayed clear of Modotti's friends and her new Stalinist circle as they housed Trotsky until he found his own home a few blocks away from the Casa Azul. It was during those months that Trotsky and Kahlo became lovers, with Rivera knowing the situation but busy with his own complicated life – Rivera knew that Frida would eventually tire of old Trotsky and so it proved to be.

By 1939 the situation in Spain was becoming chaotic and it was clear Franco's Nationalist faction would win the war as the Republicans were routed. While Franco lacked the charisma of Benito Mussolini, the moral (or physical) stature of Charles de Gaulle, the political intelligence of Franklin Roosevelt, or the rhetorical skills of Adolf Hitler, he was brutally tenacious and completely unempathic even with his own people – torturing and murdering them by the thousands – willing to achieve victory "at any price" (his own words). Modotti and Vidali had no choice but to abandon everything and move on. France for them was untenable due to political instability and heavy military deployments as by September 1939 they, along with England, were at war with Germany. The only option for the exhausted couple was a belated, depressing exit from their failed venture. They took a boat to New York knowing there was little chance of being allowed into the country. Tina Modotti was notorious.

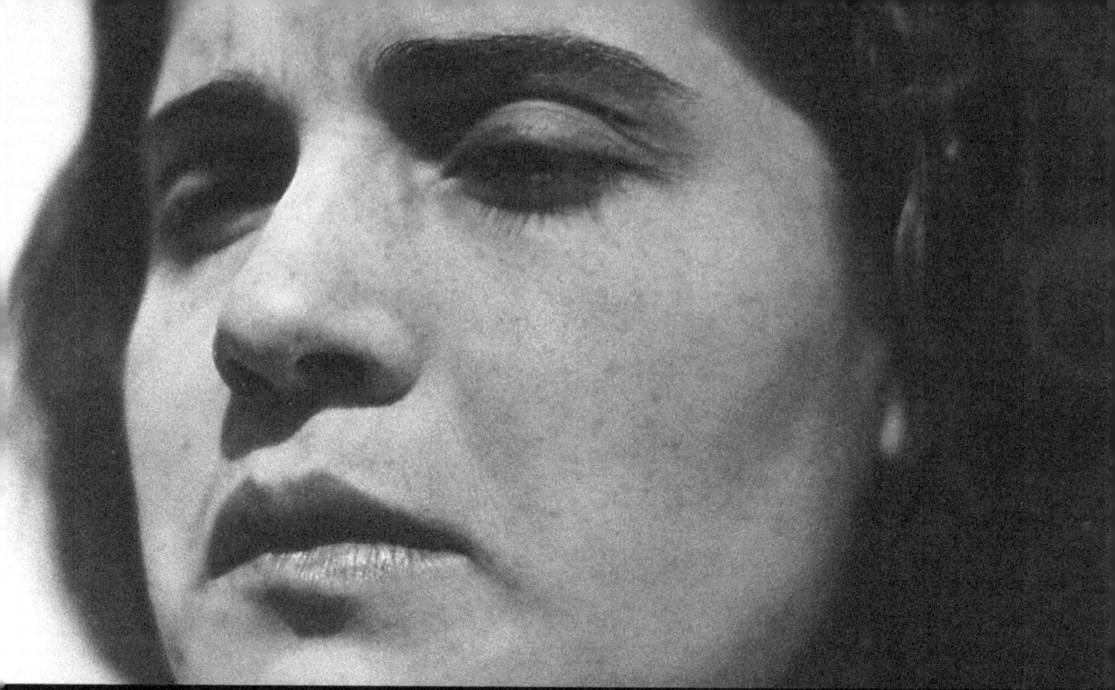

Our salvation is death, but not this one.

Franz Kafka, *The Blue and Octavo Notebooks*

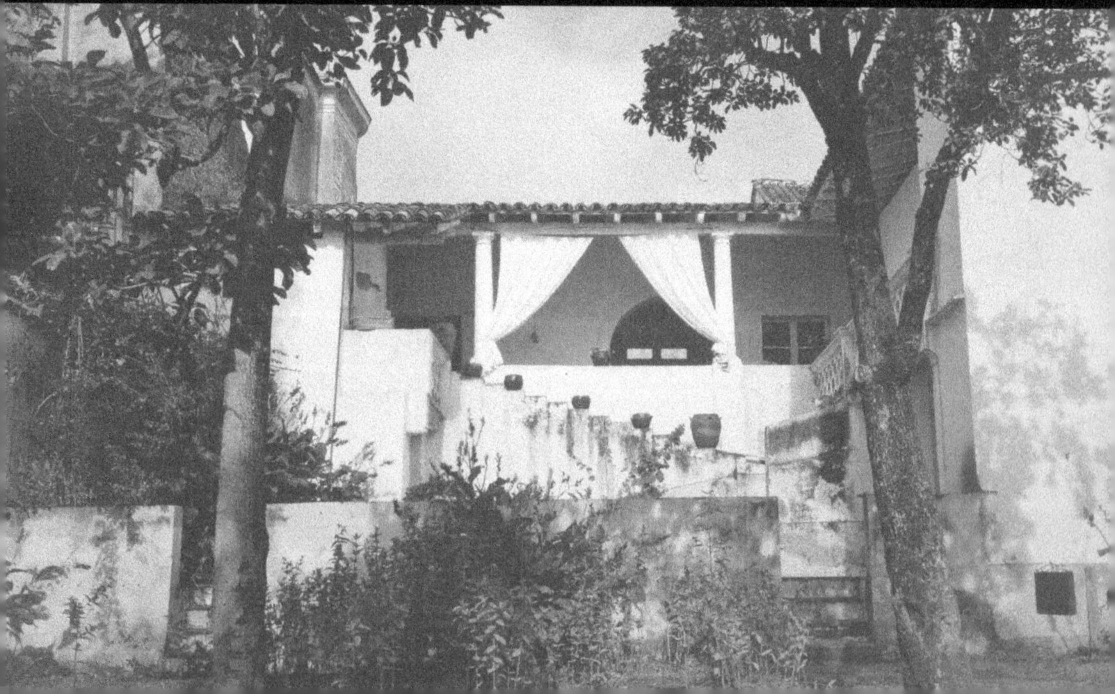

15

Mexico City Undercover

Tina Modotti: Persona Non Grata

Modotti's and Vidali's travels through war-torn Europe eventually brought them to New York where, as she suspected, she was not allowed to enter the country and was kept in isolation until her case was decided – Vidali was allowed in under a fake passport. While in isolation reporters wanted to interview and photograph the "beautiful femme fatale." They assured her that they would not discuss her politics or her history with Mella but only her beauty and possible return to Hollywood as if this would be something she would want and approve of. Modotti sent a scathing letter to Weston saying that newspapers were all obsessed with "conventions of beauty, dictated by Hollywood, while nothing else was allowed to interfere with these ideas." It seemed that nothing had changed from her days in Los Angeles.[101] Modotti moved back to Mexico City surreptitiously with Vidali's help but she was now stateless and a persona non grata.

Back in Mexico City she found a new alias, "Carmen." Using the name of Georges Bizet's eponymous femme fatale was clearly gilding the lily at this point but Modotti seems to have retained her sense of humor. She was terrified of being deported to Italy (her passport country of origin) as she was a wanted woman there and would have probably faced a mock trial and execution. She also knew that the Mexican police, inspired by fascist tactics in Europe, were on the prowl. Modotti lay low and did not contact her old friends. She tried to recover her always fragile health and worked on translations that barely paid enough to stay alive. She read the paper and listened to music on the radio keeping track of the fall of Spain to the fascists and the rising possibility of a Nazi victory in the rest of Europe.

Stalin Loses His Aura

Once the news flashed on August 24, 1939, that Stalin and Hitler had signed a nonaggression pact Modotti balked and refused to go along with the program. She realized Stalin was compromising with Hitler for the sake of power and biding his time, waiting to see who would win the war to make his next move. Strategically it was in many ways a good chess move but for many on the hard left, including Modotti, Stalin lost his superhuman glow, his "aura" – becoming just another "politico" hedging his bets and doing whatever was necessary to win.

It wasn't a matter of simply "nonaggression" – Hitler and Stalin had agreed to partition and eventually subsume the sovereign Baltic republics and Finland into their totalitarian "spheres of influence." Once Modotti turned against Stalin her own life was at risk, not only from fascist police already looking for her but also now from Soviet undercover agents with orders to kill prominent defectors. Ironically the man in charge of this in Mexico City was her companion Vittorio Vidali.

After Modotti's death some of her friends, including Diego Rivera, assumed that Vidali had killed her, being an expert in such matters and having few qualms about what needed to be done in wartime – there might even have been a sexual aspect that added a certain frisson to the task. Vidali seems like a man as much attracted to the drama of undercover work as he was to the political ideology. One can see that under slightly different circumstances he might have been a Nazi agent or an American operative. Vidali liked the "chess moves" aspect of clandestine work as much as the actual execution.

Vidali had been involved in a dramatic failed assassination attempt against Trotsky on May 12, 1940, as he and some men, with guns blazing, had unsuccessfully ambushed the Russian's heavily guarded compound in Coyoacán, a few blocks from Rivera's and Frida Kahlo's Casa Azul. The Mexican artist David Alfaro Siqueiros was involved in the failed ambush as Trotsky's heavily armed guards barely fended off the assault – Vidali's men only managed to wound Trotsky's teenage grandson Esteban Volkov in the foot. Trotsky's immediate family, with the exception of his wife, had been murdered or sent to gulags where they died and he was determined to do everything possible to keep his grandson alive. Vidali, ever the professional, escaped arrest but Siqueiros went into hiding, disguising himself (badly) as a farmer. He was easily found and arrested but due to Neruda's influence he was allowed to go into exile in Chile rather than face a long trial and prison. Siqueiros redeemed himself much later (at least as an artist) by participating in the first Mexican contingent at the XXV Venice Biennale (1950) exhibition along with José Clemente Orozco, Rufino Tamayo and Diego Rivera where they held a long overdue victory lap for the muralist movement.

Trotsky was finally assassinated in his home a year later August 20, 1940 when Stalinists managed to sneak in a harmless-looking young assistant of Spanish origin who befriended Trotsky before killing him by stabbing him in the head with an ice pick. For Diego and Frida, who might very well have been visiting the Trotsky's, as they did regularly, when the ambush occurred or when he was finally killed, there was a sense that the war was getting ever closer to home – no one could be trusted.

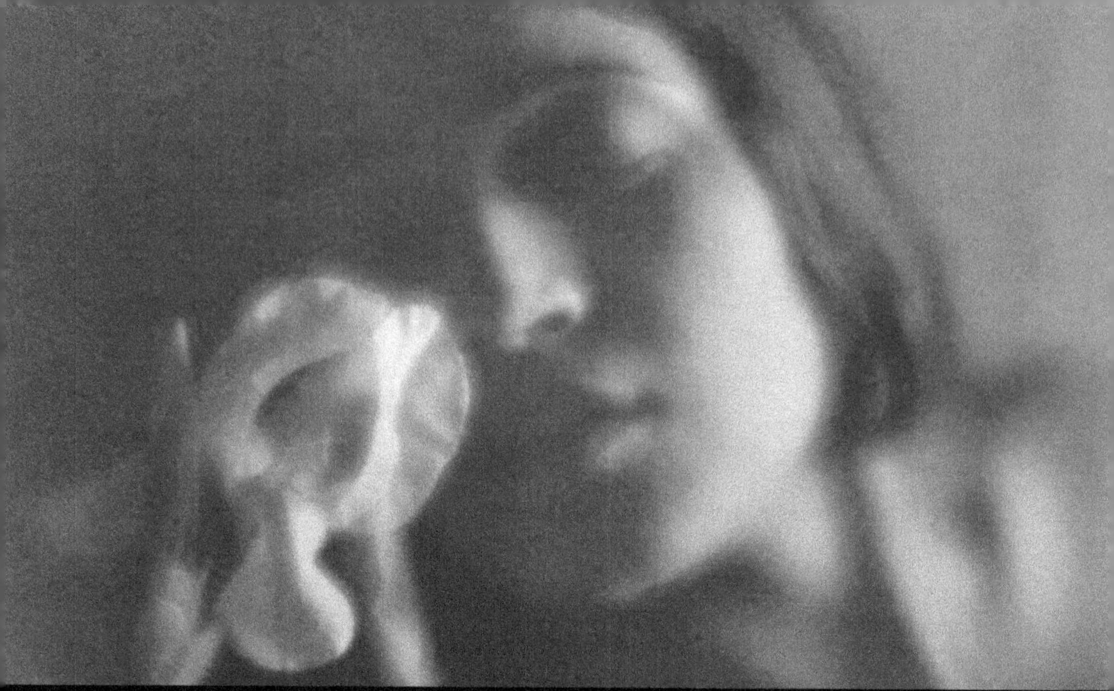

Love is so short, forgetting is so long.

Pablo Neruda, *Love Poems*

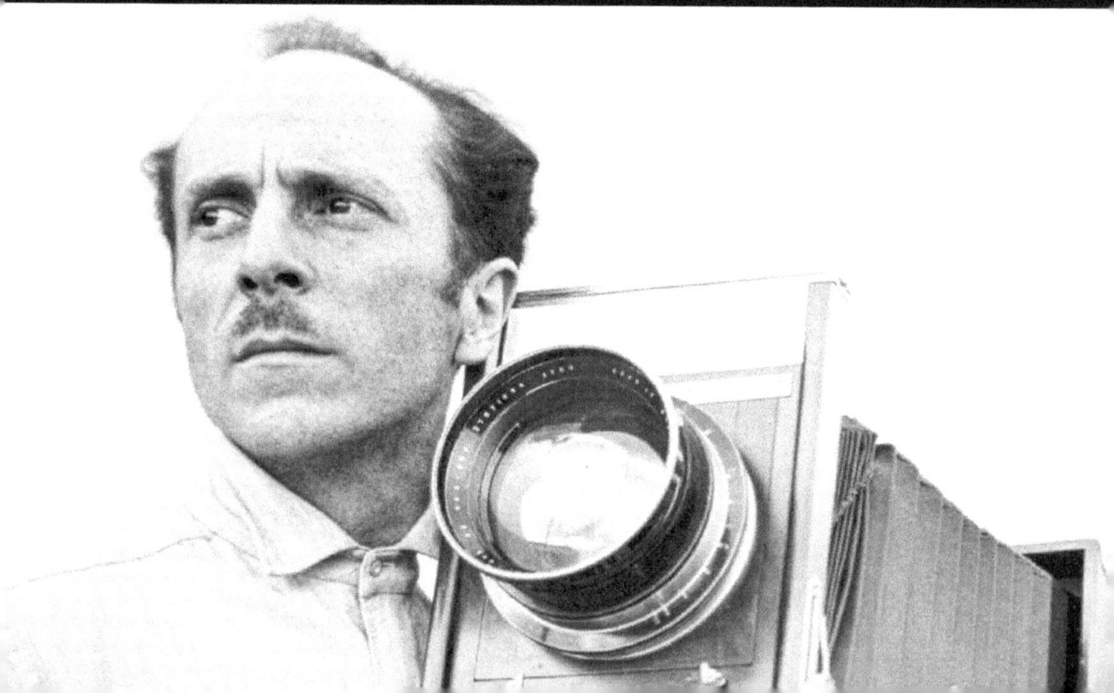

16

Tina Visits an Old Friend and Edward Remembers an Old Love

Tina Visits an Old Friend

Modotti kept to herself and began to grind out a living as a translator as knowing four languages was the marketable skill that saved her from complete poverty. She was also diagnosed as having congestive heart problems and was prescribed rest, which, undoubtedly, she refused to do, taking up volunteer work in her off hours. In one instance she, unannounced, visited her friend from her past life, Manuel Álvarez Bravo, who was not a fellow traveler but a man who went his own way politically and photographically. His work was heavily indebted to Modotti as he took up the mantle of her confluence of formalism and documentary work but took it in his own idiosyncratic "magic realist" direction with off kilter, dark, surrealist humor. She had known Bravo since he was a shy youngster asking for advice and help but too reserved to attend her *tertulias*. The trip must have been a tough one for Tina as she was determined to stay clear of old friends in the city lest she cause trouble for them or get herself arrested but she could not stay away. Bravo was not one of her close friends but he was a working photographer and that is what made the difference in this case.

Bravo recounted the meeting in an interview many years after the fact:

> "At that time I had a little studio in Ahuntamiento Street, and one day all of a sudden the bell rang. I opened and it was Tina. Well, it was a very emotional moment...then it passed. We were talking and something impressed me very much. I said to her "Tina – I have a Graflex camera and here is a darkroom." She liked that camera a lot and I had a Graflex. And then she said "No, Manuel, not now, not now." She said this very, very sadly."[102]

The sad and lonely woman who could not even face borrowing a camera or a darkroom from her old friend Bravo tells us much. In that meeting Modotti already seems like a dead woman, a ghost wandering the city looking for old places, friends and lovers – maybe for a confirmation that she had once been loved.

With her enthusiasm for Stalinism, and perhaps even for photography, waning, or already behind her, it is difficult to see what path lay ahead for the 45-year-old Modotti, but she must have realized that her heart condition and deteriorating health made those kinds of questions problematic and perhaps unnecessary. Still the question goes begging: Did Modotti lose her talent due to her religious devotion to Stalinism or did she suppress it and keep it under wraps for the sake of the cause? There is no way to know but I would guess the latter – her melancholy visit to Bravo's studio says as much – as if a part of her wanted to go back to photography (to Bravo) but she couldn't follow through. She was caught in the middle, first going to see Bravo but then refusing his help. The visit must have been emotionally draining, perhaps devastating.

Elena Poniatowska states that in an interview with the widow of Ben Traven (the leftist writer of the novel *The Treasure of the Sierra Madre*), an old friend of Modotti's, who said that she accidentally ran into Tina at this time in a Mexico City post office and she seemed very anguished and gestured for her not to approach her.[103] She was also told that Modotti met Valentín Gonzalez, aka El Campesino, a Spanish Republican military commander during the Spanish Civil War – they had met when Tina was working in field hospitals as a nurse. Valentín spoke to Modotti and told her that when they were in Spain he had decided not to kill Vidali despite what he knew about him. Reportedly Modotti replied: "You should have shot him. I hate him but have to follow him until I die."[104] Modotti did not elaborate on why a Communist with Stalinist credentials would want to kill Vidali or why she had to follow him until she died –her words are suggestive but prove nothing conclusively.

Vidali's undercover work continued after Modotti's death, taking him to Cuba, Turkey, France, and back to Spain. Like Modotti he had many names: Enea Sormenti, Jacobo Zender and Carlos Contreras. He died in 1983, only a few years before the collapse of the Soviet Union and the final end of the dream of a Marxist proletarian revolution. He always denied having had anything to do with Mella's assassination or Modotti's death and no hard evidence has ever come to light. Whatever pact he had with her was something they both took to the grave and it is unlikely we will ever know the full story.

First Name Carmen

Adelina Zendejas, a doctor of philosophy and feminist scholar and journalist who was a casual friend of Modotti during her years with Weston, met her again years later as "Carmen" in Mexico City. She was with Isabel Carbajal, whose husband was highly placed within Red Aid and a friend of Vidali's. Carbajal, knowing that Zendejas knew Modotti, asked her if she knew who this "Carmen" was. Adelina had no idea but noticed the woman had an accent. Patricia Albers picks up the story:

> "She's not Spanish, is she?"
>
> "No, she's not" replied Isabel.
>
> "No, but her voice reminds me of someone."
>
> "Come on, think Adelina."
>
> "Well, let's see Isabel. He (Carmen's partner) is Carlos Contreras (a Vidali alias) right? Then she was the wife of Julio Antonio Mella."
>
> "Yes, it's Tina Modotti."[105]

This episode makes it plain how dramatically Tina's appearance had changed, but also how loath she was to unmask herself, even to a politically compatible friend."[106] Modotti had reason to be cautious – the warring factions within the left in the city would put any Hollywood melodrama to shame in terms of narrative logic. Spanish Fascists sent from the Falangists mixed with American businessmen, and Soviet agents dressed as students mixed with Trotskyite agents dressed as professors – all in the fashionable Avenida 5 de Mayo, that had upscale shops, mainly American and European – creating a sense of the tragic/absurd worthy of Orson Welles.

For the spymaster Vidali, who enjoyed the intrigue and the danger, Mexico City was the perfect place to be, but for the social Modotti, who treasured long friendships, deep conversation, tenderness and sexual companionship, it was not any kind of a life – but true to her word she stuck it out with Vidali to the end. On January 6, 1942, her last day, she visited her friend José Clemente Orozco, whom both Weston and Modotti had befriended and photographed; she then went home to continue her translation work.

That evening she went to a dinner party with Vidali at the home of Hannes and Lena Meyer, who were "fellow travelers." The Meyers were well connected and virtual royalty within the ranks of the Party having connections not only in Europe but also in the US. Hannes, a lifelong Communist, had run the Bauhaus in Germany before Hitler's rise to power forced his emigration to the Soviet Union where he met Modotti in Moscow. After the situation with Stalin became impossible he moved to Mexico City's more temperate climate. The dinner guests also included friends Maria and Mario Montagnana, and a young artist neighbor Ignacio Aguirre. They listened to Shostakovich's Quintet in G minor and talked about it afterward with Hannes and Aguirre getting into a discussion of modern music and art. Hannes was generally upbeat about the future and tried his best to infect Tina with his positive outlook. He told her that she looked pale and sad while she had looked so healthy and full of energy at the house of Pablo Neruda just a few days earlier. Meyer later said that Tina and Vidali were distant and cold with each other and clearly uncomfortable. Vidali left early to go to his newspaper where he worked despite the late hour – Meyer never saw him again.

Traveling Light

After the dinner Modotti didn't feel well and took a taxi home telling the driver to take her to the Hospital General that was across the street from where she lived. She suffered a heart attack in the back of the car and was dead by the time the driver finally reached the destination. In her purse they found a picture of Mella. Her body was identified by her friend Adelina Zendejas – she arrived at the hospital as an autopsy was pending. Patricia Albers quotes Zendejas: "[She was] on the same cement slab, the same one, where Julio Antonio had been. She was nude, completely nude, with her perfect body, that perfect body she had, exquisite, and her face had something peaceful about it, something restful."[107]

Doctors who performed the autopsy determined that the "housewife Tina Modotti" had died by "generalized visceral congestion caused by an organic lesion of the heart." Modotti's traditional viewing took place at La Moderna, a run-down funeral parlor in the center of the city. On January 7 she was wrapped in a traditional Mexican white shroud, in an enormous black coffin, and placed in a hearse. A motorcade inched its way through Mexico City toward the Pantheon Dolores cemetery located on a hill overlooking the city, including the Colonia Juaréz area where she and Weston had first shared a studio.

People threw flowers, including her favorite calla lilies, or they performed a gesture well-known in Catholic Mexico and South America where a person kisses their open palm, then places it briefly on the coffin and then gives a salute of farewell with the same hand. Her old friends came as well as her Communist Party comrades who stood separately and avoided contact. Vidali did not attend. Some simply said "adios, Tina." On top of the coffin was an embroidered hammer and sickle, something that was a tradition for high-ranking members of the Party. Next to this embroidery was a framed photograph of Modotti – the portrait was, of course, Weston's.

It was one of his early pictures from Los Angeles simply titled *Tina, 1921*. There are a few pictures with that name but this one is a simple straightforward close-up portrait – black dress on a black background. She had kept it with her through her travels and all of her names and aliases: Assunta Adelaide Luigia Modotti Mondini. Tina de Richey. Tina Modotti-R. Maria Ruiz. Carmen. In the end she was simply Tina Modotti as inscribed on her headstone along with a poem by her friend, and fellow exile, Pablo Neruda:

> Pure your gentle name,
> pure your fragile life,
> bees, shadows, fire, snow, silence and
> foam combined with steel and wire and
> pollen to make up your firm
> and delicate being.

Neruda's dedication is beautiful and often quoted but there might be a more apt poem for the occasion by Antonio Machado, her favorite poet:

> And when the day arrives for the final voyage
> and the ship of no return is set to sail,
> you'll find me on board, traveling light...

Weston Remembers an Old Love

Weston, in the closing years of his *Daybooks* when he was living in California, remembered back to when he first heard of Modotti's death in January 1942, and started to revisit his old pictures from Los Angeles and Mexico City, and the involuntary memories they brought back to him:

> "Here is Tina in the flower of her youth. She is dressed in black, surrounded by a black background, her profile emerging from the darkness. She and Robo have been together for six years and married for four. In this photograph I have captured something too private and true and yet she is little more than a stranger to me. I immediately fell in love with her. The same photograph reached me today from Mexico. I have not seen it for twenty years. Actually, what I have before me is a photograph of Tina's bier, in which is mounted this same photograph surrounded by a wreath of flowers. Here lies Tina Modotti, a firm and delicate being. And from under the black focusing cloth it was I who created her death mask, her travel companion through her life's journey from Mexico to Germany to Russia to Spain and then back to Mexico again. Tina never asked for another one of my prints. It is as if she were aware of the significance of its final destination. Today however, I received news that she died not as a martyr but as an aging, beautiful fallen woman. The telegram said that she died of a heart attack in a Mexican taxicab. Of course, there are rumors to the contrary, probably spread by those in the Party who do not wish to see her memory die. I wonder if anyone will ever remember Tina Modotti? If they do, will they remember her beauty or her strength? I for my part can only remember her with regret. For me, she is a symbol of my utter defeat."[108]

Although these were written for his *Daybooks* they seem more like "Nightbooks" – the musings of an older man at 2 a.m. after a few drinks – one can see why he discarded the entry but at the same time one wishes for more information. For example, what did he mean by referring to Modotti as a "fallen woman" – it's highly unlikely Weston, who was not religious, suddenly saw her as "fallen" in the traditional Christian sense but what other sense is he implying? Is Modotti "beautiful and fallen" in the sense that she never found her way in the world despite her talent, intelligence, and beauty? What does he mean when he speaks of his "utter defeat?" It is unlikely that he is referring to his defeat in the photographic or artistic sense – that leaves his defeat as a man. Interestingly he considers Tina not the cause of this "utter defeat" but a "symbol" of it. Since there are no more details we will never know but the text is certainly suggestive.

Tina, 1921 was from the time they were first, tentatively, a couple and were in the process of discovering and exploring "Edward and Tina." For Weston it was a memory of love at first sight. For Modotti that picture must have been a talisman from happier days when the discoveries and the adventures were still in front of her. It is incredible that she managed to hold on to it after all of those clandestine trips with fake passports, the stays in the homes of fellow travelers, the sudden moves to new quarters, the stopovers in cheap hotels, buses, cafés, and train stations, after all of that she was unable to let that one picture go, but one understands why. Aside from being a masterpiece of portrait photography it was also the beginning of "Tina Modotti." As her friends who found the picture realized it was only right that it was there at the end – as Weston described it the picture was "her travel companion."

George Porcari

George Porcari was born in Lima, Peru in 1952. He attended Catholic school, becoming an altar boy, which he very much disliked. His favorite activities in San Isidro were going to the nearby beaches, climbing the nearby olive trees, making art, and watching television, preferably Westerns. In 1962 the family emigrated to Gardena, a working-class suburb in the South Bay section of Los Angeles. The family arrived at the same moment as the Cuban missile crisis that Porcari watched on television without much interest, preferring *The Rifleman, Dobie Gillis and The Twilight Zone*.

Porcari attended Gardena High School, which was then a Vo-Tech (vocational-technical) school where one could major in various trades – Porcari's major was auto repair. After graduating in 1970 he got various jobs, including unloading trucks – where he joined the Teamsters Union. Sometimes the jobs were in factories, department stores, or in garages. In this period he was taking pictures, in the style of Garry Winogrand and Robert Frank, two favorites at the time, but in color, using positive or slide film. He also made a short Super-8mm film, *Greetings From LA, 1978!* before moving to New York City the following year.

In New York he lived on Delancey Street near the Williamsburg Bridge. On the ground floor was a bodega run by Puerto Ricans that played their raucous music day and night, at the corner was a Vietnamese restaurant that was open late so useful for late evening lunches – nearby there was an outdoor market that sold live chickens which gives some idea of the place – not simply different but better in every sense from what it has sadly become. After a few false starts his first real job was working for the Strand Bookstore, eventually helping the book buyer. In 1984 Porcari returned to Los Angeles to attend the Art Center College of Design in Pasadena where he received his MFA and also got a job as the book-buyer for the library (thanks to that Strand job). He retired as Acquisitions Librarian after 29 years at the age of 65 – a job he often referred to as "the greatest job of all time."

Porcari has been exhibiting his photography and collage work since his first exhibit at the *Laurie Rubin Gallery* in New York City in 1988. The most recent exhibit of his art was at the *As Is Gallery* in Los Angeles of still life photographs of books. In 2016 the *Haphazard Gallery* in Los Angeles published a catalog for an exhibit of his photo work and collages titled *Greetings From LA: 24 Frames and Fifty Years* also designed (like this book) by Karen Davison. In 2018 he published a book on the work of Michelangelo Antonioni titled *The Antonioni Adventure*. The following year he published a book, in collaboration with the poet Bruna Mori, titled *Beige*, that incorporated photographs of suburbia with poetry and memoirs. In 2025 he published *The Biggest Film Biographer in the World: The Films of Ken Russell.*

At the beginning of 2024 Porcari moved to Lima, Peru to start a new chapter that remains unwritten.

Endnotes

1 Beth Gates Warren, *Artful Lives, Edward Weston, Margrethe Mather, and the Bohemians of Los Angeles,* Getty Press, 2011

2 Patricia Albers, *Shadows, Fire, Snow: The Life of Tina Modotti*, Potter, 1999

3 Anita Brenner, *Avant-Garde Art and Artists in Mexico: Anita Brenner's Journals of the Roaring Twenties*, University of Texas Press, 2010

4 Anita Brenner, *Avant-Garde Art and Artists in Mexico: Anita Brenner's Journals of the Roaring Twenties*

5 Amy Conger, *Edward Weston in Mexico 1923-1926*, San Francisco Museum of Modern Art, 1983

6 Amy Conger, *Edward Weston in Mexico 1923-1926*

7 Patricia Albers, *Shadows, Fire, Snow: The Life of Tina Modotti*

8 Ben Maddow, *Edward Weston: His Life,* Aperture, 2005

9 Margaret Hooks, *Tina Modotti: Photographer & Revolutionary,* La Fabrica, 1993

10 Patricia Albers, *Shadows, Fire, Snow: The Life of Tina Modotti*

11 Patricia Albers, *Shadows, Fire, Snow: The Life of Tina Modotti*

12 D.H. Kahnweiler, *Cubism*, Faber & Faber, 1959

13 Virginia Woolf, *Mr. Bennett and Mrs. Brown, Selected Essays*, Oxford 2009

14 Ben Maddow, *Edward Weston: His Life*

15 Margaret Hooks, *Tina Modotti: Photographer & Revolutionary*

16 Patricia Albers, *Shadows, Fire, Snow: The Life of Tina Modotti*

17 Beth Gates Warren, *Artful Lives, Edward Weston, Margrethe Mather, and the Bohemians of Los Angeles*

18 Beth Gates Warren, *Artful Lives, Edward Weston, Margrethe Mather, and the Bohemians of Los Angeles*

19 Beth Gates Warren, *Artful Lives, Edward Weston, Margrethe Mather, and the Bohemians of Los Angeles*

20 Margaret Hooks, *Tina Modotti: Photographer & Revolutionary*

21 Matthew Bernstein, *Team of Giants: The Making of the Spanish-American War,* University of Oklahoma Press, 2024

[22] Andrew Riley, *Rancheros, Revolution and Newsreels: How William Randolph Hearst's Media Empire Shaped American Involvement in the Mexican Revolution*, Senior Seminar, Academia.edu, 2014
[23] Frank McLynn, *Villa and Zapata: a History of the Mexican Revolution*, Carroll & Graf, 2000
[24] Frank McLynn, *Villa and Zapata: a History of the Mexican Revolution*
[25] Frank McLynn, *Villa and Zapata: a History of the Mexican Revolution*
[26] Joseé Carlos Mariategui, *Antologia-Seleccion*, Indroducion Martin Bergel, Siglo XXI Editorial, 2021
[27] Patricia Albers, *Shadows, Fire, Snow: The Life of Tina Modotti*
[28] Margaret Hooks, *Tina Modotti: Photographer & Revolutionary*
[29] Margaret Hooks, *Tina Modotti: Photographer & Revolutionary*
[30] Patricia Albers, *Shadows, Fire, Snow: The Life of Tina Modotti*
[31] Margaret Hooks, *Tina Modotti: Photographer & Revolutionary*
[32] Amy Conger, *Edward Weston in Mexico 1923-1926*
[33] Patricia Albers, *Shadows, Fire, Snow: The Life of Tina Modotti*
[34] Edward Weston, *The Daybooks of Edward Weston 1. Mexico*, Aperture, 1973
[35] Margaret Hooks, *Tina Modotti: Photographer & Revolutionary*
[36] Oscar Montero, (film) *Miradas Sobre Mexico: Tina Modotti*, UNAM, 1993
[37] Margaret Hooks, *Tina Modotti: Photographer & Revolutionary*
[38] Margaret Hooks, *Tina Modotti: Photographer & Revolutionary*
[39] Margaret Hooks, *Tina Modotti: Photographer & Revolutionary*
[40] Margaret Hooks, *Tina Modotti: Photographer & Revolutionary*
[41] Edward Weston, *The Daybooks of Edward Weston 1. Mexico*
[42] Edward Weston, *The Daybooks of Edward Weston 1. Mexico*
[43] José Antonio Rodriguez, *The Rupturing Gaze*, from *Tina Modotti & Edward Weston: The Mexican Years*, Throckmorton Fine Art, 1999
[44] José Antonio Rodriguez, *The Rupturing Gaze*, from *Tina Modotti & Edward Weston: The Mexican Years*
[45] Margaret Hooks, *Tina Modotti: Photographer & Revolutionary*
[46] Patricia Albers, *Shadows, Fire, Snow: The Life of Tina Modotti*
[47] Patricia Albers, *Shadows, Fire, Snow: The Life of Tina Modotti*
[48] Patricia Albers, *Shadows, Fire, Snow: The Life of Tina Modotti*
[49] Richard Morgan, *The Frida Kahlo Scandal: Fridamania Could Reach New Heights Today, but Where Are Her Missing Masterpieces?* The Guardian, 20, November, 2025
[50] Laura Mulvey, Peter Wollen, *Frida Kahlo and Tina Modotti*, Whitechapel Gallery, 1982
[51] Laura Mulvey, Peter Wollen, *Frida Kahlo and Tina Modotti*

52 Mariana Figarella: *Edward Weston y Tina Modotti en México: Su Intercion Dentro de las Estrategias Esteticas del Arte Postrevolucionario*, Universidad Nacional Autonoma de México, 2002
53 Edward Weston, *The Daybooks of Edward Weston 1. Mexico*
54 Mariana Figarella: *Edward Weston y Tina Modotti ex México: Su Intercion Dentro de las Estrategias Esteticas del Arte Postrevolucionario*
55 Andrea Noble, *Tina Modotti: Image, Texture, Photography*, University of New Mexico, 2000
56 John Crosse, *Edward Weston Remembers Tina Modotti, January 1942*, Southern California Architectural History (Blog), 2011
57 Patricia Albers, *Shadows, Fire, Snow: The Life of Tina Modotti*
58 Edward Weston, *The Daybooks of Edward Weston 1. Mexico*
59 Margaret Hooks, *Tina Modotti: Photographer & Revolutionary*
60 John Crosse, *Edward Weston Remembers Tina Modotti, January 1942*
61 Elena Poniatowska, *Tinísima*, Seix Barral, 2016
62 José Maria Peña, *Tomorrow Closes the Magnificent Exposition of Edward Weston and Tina Modotti*, Documents of Latin American and Latino Art, International Center for the Americas at the Museum of Fine Arts, Houston, 1925
63 Patricia Albers, *Shadows, Fire, Snow: The Life of Tina Modotti*
64 John Crosse, *Edward Weston Remembers Tina Modotti, January 1942*
65 Edward Weston, *The Daybooks of Edward Weston 1. Mexico*
66 Patricia Albers, *Shadows, Fire, Snow: The Life of Tina Modotti*
67 Giorgio Agamben, *Creation and Anarchy: The Work of Art and the Religion of Capitalism*, Stanford, 2019
68 Edward Weston, *The Daybooks of Edward Weston 1. Mexico*
69 Edward Weston, *Edward Weston, His Life and Photographs*, Aperture, 1979
70 Mary Street Alinder, *Group f.64: Edward Weston, Ansel Adams, Imogen Cunningham and the Community of Artists Who Revolutionized American Photography*, Bloomsbury, 2014
71 Edward Weston, *Edward Weston, His Life and Photographs*
72 Edward Weston, *Edward Weston, His Life and Photographs*
73 Sean O'Hagan, *Edward Weston: The Greatest American Photographer of His Generation?* The Guardian, 18, August, 2010
74 Elena Poniatowska, translation George Porcari, *Tinisima*, Seix Barral, 2016
75 Margaret Hooks, *Tina Modotti: Photographer & Revolutionary*
76 Isabe Tejeda Martin, *The Critical Fortunes of Tina Modotti*, from *Tina Modotti*, Prestel, 2024
77 Lewis Hine, *America and Lewis Hine: Photographs 1904-1940*, Aperture, 1997
78 Simone de Beauvoir, "The Positive Aspect of Ambiguity," *The Ethics of Ambiguity*, Citadel Press, 1976

79 Margaret Hooks, *Tina Modotti: Photographer & Revolutionary*
80 Lucy Moore, *Anything Goes, A Biography of the Roaring Twenties*, Overlook, 2010
81 Margaret Hooks, *Tina Modotti: Photographer & Revolutionary*
82 Jesús Nieto Sotelo, Elisa Lozano Alvarez, *Tina Modotti: A New Vision, 1929*, CNCA/Centro de la Imagen, 2000
83 Jesús Nieto Sotelo, Elisa Lozano Alvarez, *Tina Modotti: A New Vision, 1929*
84 Jesús Nieto Sotelo, Elisa Lozano Alvarez, *Tina Modotti: A New Vision, 1929*
85 Jesús Nieto Sotelo, Elisa Lozano Alvarez, *Tina Modotti: A New Vision, 1929*
86 Jesús Nieto Sotelo, Elisa Lozano Alvarez, *Tina Modotti: A New Vision, 1929*
87 Jesús Nieto Sotelo, Elisa Lozano Alvarez, *Tina Modotti: A New Vision, 1929*
88 Jesús Nieto Sotelo, Elisa Lozano Alvarez, *Tina Modotti: A New Vision, 1929*
89 Amy Stark (ed.), *The Letters From Tina Modotti to Edward Weston*, The Archive, Research Series Number 22, January 1986
90 Patricia Albers, *Shadows, Fire, Snow: The Life of Tina Modotti*
91 Patricia Albers, *Shadows, Fire, Snow: The Life of Tina Modotti*
92 Anita Brenner, *Avant-Garde Art and Artists in Mexico: Anita Brenner's Journals of the Roaring Twenties*, University of Texas, 2010
93 Laura Mulvey, Peter Wollen, *Frida Kahlo and Tina Modotti*, Whitechapel Gallery, 1982
94 Margaret Hooks, *Tina Modotti: Photographer & Revolutionary*
95 Margaret Hooks, *Tina Modotti: Photographer & Revolutionary*
96 Patricia Albers, *Shadows, Fire, Snow: The Life of Tina Modotti*
97 Martin Amis, *Koba the Dread: Laughter and the Twenty Million*, Hyperion, 2002
98 Martin Amis, *Koba the Dread: Laughter and the Twenty Million*
99 Oksana Bulgakowa, *Sergei Eisenstein, A Biography*, Potemking Press, 1998
100 Patricia Albers, *Shadows, Fire, Snow: The Life of Tina Modotti*
101 Laura Mulvey, Peter Wollen, *Frida Kahlo and Tina Modotti*
102 Patricia Albers, *Shadows, Fire, Snow: The Life of Tina Modotti*
103 Elena Poniatowska, Interview, *Miradas Sobre Mexico: Tina Modotti 1896-1942*, (Film), Alejandro Islas, Oscar Montero, Adriana Garcia, 1980
104 Margaret Hooks, *Tina Modotti: Photographer & Revolutionary*
105 Patricia Albers, *Shadows, Fire, Snow: The Life of Tina Modotti*
106 Patricia Albers, *Shadows, Fire, Snow: The Life of Tina Modotti*
107 Patricia Albers, *Shadows, Fire, Snow: The Life of Tina Modotti*
108 John Crosse, *Edward Weston Remembers Tina Modotti, January 1942*

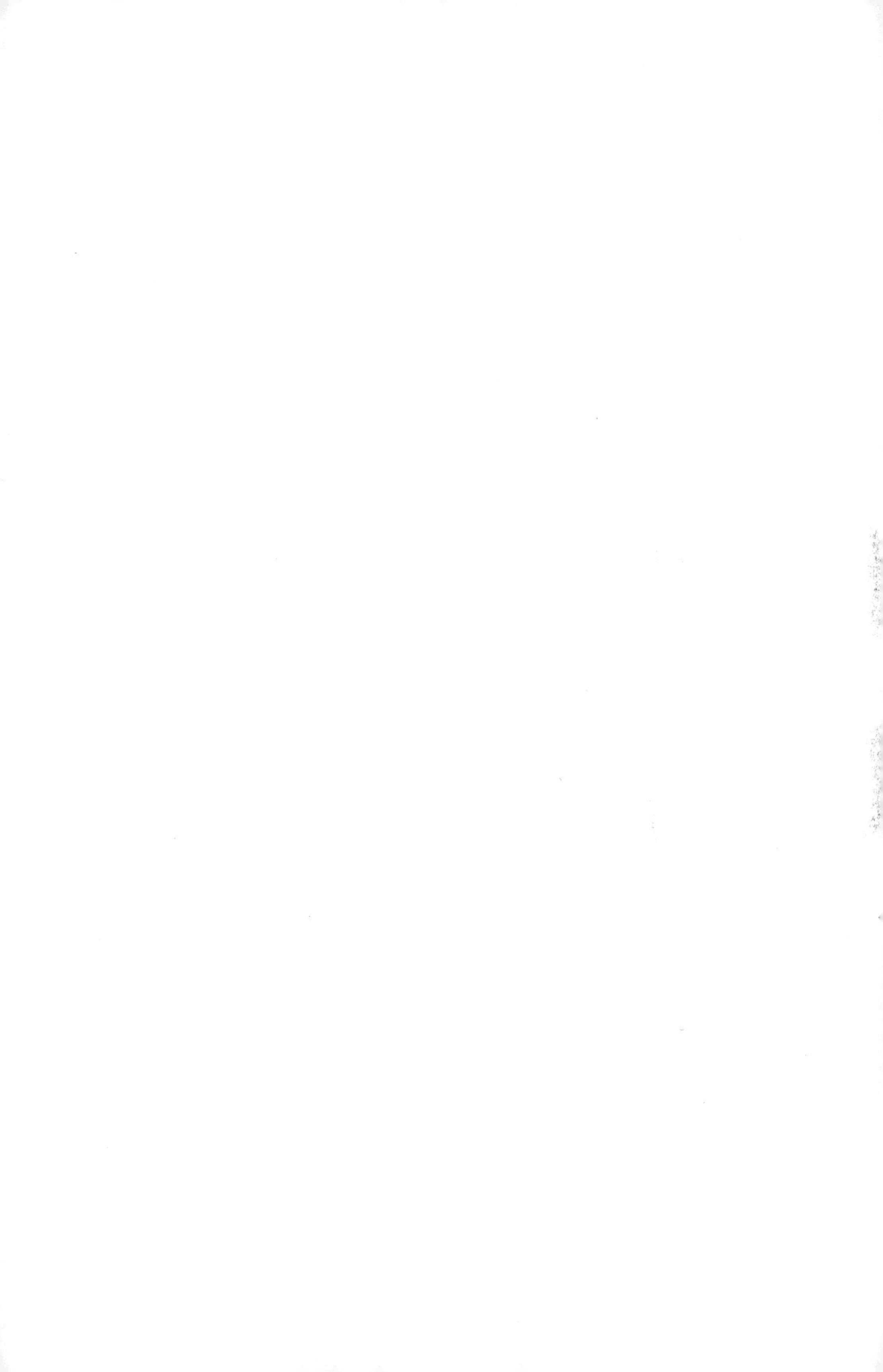

www.ingramcontent.com/pod-product-compliance
Ingram Content Group UK Ltd.
Pitfield, Milton Keynes, MK11 3LW, UK
UKHW061133310726
14090UKWH00036B/1004

9 798234 015044